Key Business Concepts

Key Business Concepts

A concise guide

Bengt Karlöf
Translated by Allan J. Gilderson

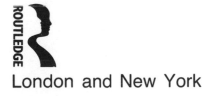

London and New York

First published 1993
by Routledge
11 New Fetter Lane, London EC4P 4EE

Simultaneously published in the USA and Canada
by Routledge
29 West 35th Street New York, NY 10001

Phototypeset in Baskerville by
Intype, London

Printed and bound in Great Britain by
Mackays of Chatham PLC, Chatham, Kent

British Library Cataloguing in Publication Data

A catalogue record for this book is available from the British Library.

Library of Congress Cataloging in Publication Data

Karlöf, Bengt, 1939–
Key business concepts: a concise guide/Bengt Karlöf.
p. cm.
Translated from Swedish.
Simultaneously published in the USA and Canada.
Includes bibliographical references and index.

ISBN 0–415–08853–4

1. Business – Dictionaries. I. Title.
HF1001.K37 1993
650'.03 – dc20 92–30210 CIP

ISBN 0–415–08853–4 (pbk)

Contents

Figures

Tables

Preface

The turbulent economic history of the 1970s and 1980s has generated a strong growth of interest in the factors that influence a company's business development. The ability of old models and creeds to explain events was found to be much less than had previously been believed, and many approaches originating in the heyday of planning technocracy simply had to be scrapped. Concentration on resource management gave way to concern for the customer and for customers' need structures as the starting point of all business activity, and it was discovered that subtle components difficult to quantify had a strong bearing on the development of companies and their business.

In such situations where new knowledge is needed to replace old knowledge that is no longer valid, one always sees the rise of many new ideas, models and concepts which are often only vaguely defined. The past decade offers a textbook example of the search for new models and the bandying about of new and ill-defined terms. Parodists call this 'corporate bullshit', but that epithet should properly be applied to the way the terms are used rather than to the concepts as such. They can also be viewed as an expression of outsiders' ignorance as to the exact meanings of the terms. If somebody talks about 'vertical integration' or the need to 'build entry barriers', it sounds to the uninitiated as if he is throwing up a smokescreen to avoid discussion of concrete issues.

This book was originally initiated by the Scandinavian Airlines System in 1987. SAS felt a need for a concise guide to concepts and models for their business training of executives. What was originally planned as a glossary turned into a book that has been continuously re-written and expanded.

Apparently there is a worldwide need for this type of publication. The book has now been translated into no less than fourteen languages including quite exotic ones like Russian and Japanese. Let me hope that it will contribute to efficiency improvements in industry and the

public sector. Any suggestions for improvements will be thankfully
received.

Bengt Karlöf
Stockholm

Introduction

CONTEMPORARY TRENDS

A well-known historian said recently that epochs in human history do not, as we tend to believe, coincide with calendar centuries and decades. He maintained that the nineteenth century did not really end until the outbreak of World War I in 1914. The twentieth century, on the other hand, came to an early end in 1991 with the collapse of the planned economies of Eastern Europe, the fall of the Berlin Wall and the disintegration of the Soviet Union.

People always tend to believe that they are living at a turning-point in history, a shift of paradigm or whatever you like to call it. The question is, however, whether the 1990s are not in fact the dawn of a new age in which the concept of efficiency will dominate both business life and other forms of organized activity. The planned economies of Eastern Europe have proved inefficient in satisfying two primary human requirements, economic prosperity and personal liberty. Political systems that fail to provide their citizens with these basics are doomed to collapse. Similarly, companies and organizations cannot continue to exist unless they produce a perceived utility in relation to the resources (cost and capital) which they consume.

This apparently self-evident truth has not been all that widely recognized in Europe. The whole ongoing process of European integration is in fact an example of a system striving for greater efficiency. That term, in this context, refers to value (utility) created as a function of price. The aim of all business is to create something whose value is greater than the cost of producing it. (For a fuller discussion, see Efficiency, p. 75)

Non-profit and co-operative organizations equate value with cost. If value, measured in income, exceeds costs, the price is reduced to cancel out the profit. In the reverse case, the organization comes under financial pressure or loses members, compelling it to take some sort of action.

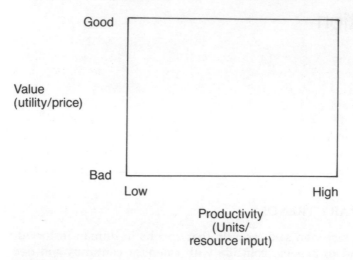

Figure 1 Efficiency matrix

The feedback system in planned-economy organizations is much more diffuse. The term planned economy as used here means a unit that derives its resources not from customers or other users, but from an allocating authority. In addition to public-sector bodies, most functional departments within private-sector companies exist in a planned economy, in so far as their resources are allocated to them by the corporate management; the internal 'customers' to whom they deliver are not free to choose other suppliers.

The efficiency matrix shown above is parallel to the Value Graph.
I have used this simple diagram many times to illustrate the difference between productivity and efficiency. This is a difference that is often not understood. The Trabant, that little East German car, is an excellent example. Let us suppose as a hypothesis that *productivity* in the manufacture of that car had been exceptionally high – say thirty-five man-hours per vehicle, a Japanese world championship class figure. Yet the *efficiency* of production would still have been low because few people, given a free choice, would pay money for a Trabant (even though it has become something of a cult object and collector's piece since production was discontinued). Thus we can paradoxically define a planned economy as a system that is not even capable of producing what nobody wants to buy.

Efficiency, then, is the quotient between utility and price. This is the very essence of business acumen.

EUROPE AS AN ILLUSTRATIVE EXAMPLE

Europe represents one-third of the Western world, and for the past couple of decades it has been the one-third that has fallen farthest behind in economic growth, unemployment, etc. The fact is that Europe possesses a tremendous potential for efficiency. The public sector is the area that is easiest to identify in this respect. Each country has its own administration, its own civil aviation authority, department of education, bank regulators, and so on. The result is not only low productivity in the public sector, but also inefficiency due to a shortage of qualified people, especially in the smaller countries. The instinct for organizational self-preservation precludes a civil aviation or education authority in a small Scandinavian country, for example, from shutting down its operations and buying those services from the country next door instead.

Public-sector systems thus constitute a gigantic potential for rationalization in Europe. The mere fact that each country has its own currency represents a charge of about 0.6 per cent against Europe's aggregate GDP; that is what it costs to pay all the people in banks and bureaux de change who make a living by trading currencies. If all the irrationalities in European public administration are added up, the potential gains from rationalization are mind-boggling.

The situation in industry is even more serious. Historically, European business has derived enormous benefit for centuries past from its fragmented national structure. Ever since the age of mercantilism, many industries and trading houses have existed in symbiosis with the State, and this has encouraged healthy competition between different national systems. The whole idea of mercantilism was to procure cheap raw materials that could be resold, maybe in processed form, to generate a surplus that the nations could use to finance Europe's incessant wars. However grotesque it may seem in retrospect, this system undeniably promoted competition which for a long time benefited the development of Europe.

In the twentieth century, however, the fragmented structure of Europe has led to serious disadvantages. This does not apply so much to small industrialized countries like the Netherlands, Switzerland and Sweden. The leading industrialists in those countries realized long ago that their domestic markets were too small to allow them to benefit from economies of scale. The situation is much worse in medium to large countries like France, Britain and Italy. Their industries face enormous difficulties because they have for too long been content to regard their own national markets as synonymous with the market served.

Economies of scale, i.e. distribution of fixed costs over a large number of units produced, are totally dependent on the relationship between fixed costs, organizational efficiency and the size of the market served. Companies like Bull in France, Vickers in Britain and many more like them have been hit hard by competition from Japanese, South-East Asian and American companies. The fragmented national structure that for centuries was the key to success has thus turned into an obstacle to the further development of the European continent. Hopefully this has now been realized, and the realization, together with the unshackling of Eastern Europe, could be the shot in the arm that gets the Old World moving forward again.

The definition of efficiency as the quotient between utility functions and price also clearly implies that successful operation in any field, and perhaps most of all in business, requires a constant balancing of the sum of utility functions against the price demanded for them. Different customers, naturally enough, put different values on a given utility function. This is the very basis of all segmentation. It also means that customers grouped in segments exhibit varying degrees of willingness to pay for different utility functions.

This whole line of argument leads to the conclusion that business-manship is a matter of weighing utility functions segment by segment against the cost of producing them and how much customers are prepared to pay for them. All this is extremely complicated from the standpoint of the private individual.

People vary. Some of us feel most comfortable with countable quantities, while others enjoy serving customers. The ability to balance utility functions against costs within the compass of a single human brain is not at all common, and this helps to explain the rarity of excellent leaders and the high remuneration that successful ones command in the business world.

The efficiency matrix expresses this in terms of productivity as a function of quality, where quality is the sum of utility functions. The Japanese have taught people in many parts of the world how to combine the advantages of economies of scale and those of the Experience Curve with a high degree of individual customer utility. Let me give you an example of the opposite.

A few years ago I was informed that our friendly neighbourhood post office in a suburb of Stockholm was to be closed. Since a fairly extensive municipal planning programme was already well advanced and redevelopment had already begun, I wrote to the postmaster general asking why this had happened. He sent me a courteous reply explaining that the local post office was not profitable enough to justify its continued existence. I wrote back, tongue in cheek, noting how easy it was to make a calculation showing that a post office ought to be closed down. As an economist: myself, I could easily have done the same sums. I suggested that the Post Office, in its capacity as a national monopoly, ought to close all its branches except one in Stockholm, to which people from all over the country could come to collect their mail. My counterproposal was that he should make a more intelligent analysis to identify those parts of the value chain where advantages of scale were to be gained and those where the greatest customer utility was to be found, and then to try and strike an optimum balance between rational production and customer utility. In reply I received a handsome stamp album accompanied by a business card with a cordial greeting, whereupon the dialogue came to an end.

It is of course easy for non-competitive systems to optimize their economies – or believe that that is what they are doing. Toyota was one of the pioneers who showed the world the analytical way to approach an optimum balance between customer satisfaction and economies of scale. Let us learn from each other, especially from the Japanese.

There are a number of points that have governed traditional strategic thinking in the United States:

1 A large, integrated market.
2 The Experience Curve.
3 Advantages of scale.
4 High market shares and long production runs.
5 Competition by price.

The obverse side of this tradition is a high degree of cost-effectiveness and fierce price competition, leading to high efficiency in terms of costs. The reverse side, on the other hand, is reflected in rather humdrum products, little customization, lack of variety and low quality. It must be added that the trend in the United States is now changing; however, what we are talking about here is the strategic heritage, not the situation as of 1993.

Europe, by contrast, has a tradition of:

1 A fragmented market where the value put on utility functions varies.
2 Strong differentiation and relatively high quality.
3 Nations synonymous with markets.
4 Short production runs and high prices.
5 Differentiated products as a result of competition by customization.

Up-market cars like the Jaguar, Mercedes, BMW and Saab are all examples of this tradition, whose obverse side is traditional quality with a high degree of adaptation to customers' needs (utility functions). The generally high level of quality is reflected for example in the long lifetime of cars. Here the reverse side is composed of short production runs, high costs and differentiation rather than price as the chief competitive weapon, leading to loss of competitive ability in mass-market segments.

The foregoing description is over-simplified; as I mentioned earlier, European industry is or ought to be moving towards higher productivity and competition by price.

It is fair to say that the Japanese have taught both Americans and Europeans the art of integrating a high degree of customer utility with high productivity – in other words, efficiency. This is the very essence of strategic efficiency. Systems that are shielded from competition will certainly take much longer to learn it than producers, especially of goods, who have to face competition. Producers of services, rather than producers of goods, are likely to be most affected by the business challenge of the future.

STRATEGIC AS OPPOSED TO OPERATIVE EFFICIENCY

The term strategy was over-exploited in the 1980s, a time when the behaviour of many people was far from strategic. A friend of mine recently remarked that 'the word strategy is used nowadays as soon as anybody thinks before he does something.' In the 1980s it was debased to mean any thought that preceded action, regardless of the length or breadth of view involved. As used in this book, the word strategy refers to a long-term, overriding pattern of action to make progress in a direction that will assure the continued existence and prosperity of an enterprise.

When we speak of the *strategy development process*, we mean the process of

1 Defining a development mission for a portfolio or a corporate mission for a business unit.
2 Staking out an overall pattern of actions designed to promote the long-term survival of the enterprise.
3 Setting goals for the speed and extent of progress in the desired direction.

In the stable world of technocratic management, ends took precedence over means. The order of precedence now depends on circumstances. If the task is to expel Iraqi troops from Kuwait, then the goal is more important than the strategy. But in a turbulent world, the direction of travel is often more important than the destination. The latter, in such cases, is simply a datum point by which to measure progress in the desired direction.

If we want to decide on our order of priorities, we can make a breakdown of strategic and operative skills something like this:

Strategic efficiency	*Operative efficiency*
1 Products	1 Costs
2 Markets	2 Capital
3 Applications	3 Quality
4 Competitive position	4 Productivity
5 Profitability and growth	5 Functional efficiency
6 Bottom Line	6 Profits

Choice of products in the broadest sense of the term, i.e. the mix of goods and services offered to the market, is an important strategic issue with almost infinite possibilities for gaining a competitive edge.

The choice of markets may seem trivial but actually involves a question of decisive importance to business, that of segmentation, together with the associated question of differentiation in the form of the aforementioned product mix.

Application is actually a special case of segmentation. Position relative to competitors, the choice between high profitability or long or short-term growth, as well as price elasticity of demand (i.e. the willingness of customers in different segments to pay and the adoption of appropriate pricing policies), are other important strategic considerations. These considerations affect business units. Portfolio strategy also includes choice of industries to operate in, acquisitions and divestments, synergies, etc.

Operative issues are narrower in scope and shorter in perspective. Strategists generally tend to underrate the value of operative skills. Given good operative management, a company has a good chance of avoiding the kind of acute problems that generally hurt much more than adjustments of a proactive nature. If General Motors or Scandinavian Airline Systems had done something constructive about their cost position during the good years, they would have saved themselves the necessity of making painful structural changes when the recession came.

Unfortunately there is a strong tendency during boom times to look askance at operative ability. Yet that is perhaps just when operative skills are most valuable. Discerning corporate executives ought to be aware of this paradoxical tendency of the business cycle to encourage counterproductive leadership. Upswings encourage a flamboyant, visionary and expansive style of leadership at the expense of strategic precision and operative skill. When things are going well, you do not earn yourself a reputation by griping about productivity and tied-up capital.

Table 1 lists some important criteria or archetypes for assessing the condition of an enterprise. It is headed 'typology of efficiency' because it covers both strategic and operative aspects. It deals with the 'hard' components of business, hardly touching at all upon the often important aspect of organizational efficiency.

Table 1 Typology of efficiency for companies

Industry	Competition	Inward efficiency
Growth	Actors	Capital
Trade logic	Profitability	Costs
Profitability	Customer-perceived	Productivity
Subtleties	quality	Functional efficiency
Segments	Loyalty	Culture
Success factors	Cost position	
	Motivation	
	Pricing	

In all contexts dealing with whole companies it is necessary to draw a line, which means discarding something. Business management and business control are special in that they cut right across many of the traditional boundaries between areas of knowledge, dealing with such things as:

- economics
- technology
- psychology
- sociology
- jurisprudence
- etc.

Business ability, and the long-term variant thereof known as strategic ability, cannot in my opinion be assigned to any particular subject field but are interdisciplinary phenomena.

SOME TRENDS IN THE FIELD OF STRATEGY

During the 1980s the subject of strategy was discussed from two principal standpoints. The first aspect which was strongly emphasized was that of competition. The chief representative of this standpoint is Michael Porter, who in several excellent books has continued to develop the Harvard tradition with its basically deterministic view and consequent analytical approach. Porter's three books *Competitive Strategy, Competitive Advantage* and *Competitive Advantage of Nations* emphasize the importance of competition in business and national dynamics. The planning technocrat's preference for structural solutions aimed at eliminating or reducing competition has turned out to be an approach of very dubious value in the long term.

The second aspect, which we can call that of organization, has Henry

Mintzberg and David Hussey as its main proponents. Mintzberg, in his article 'Crafting Strategy' (1987), has emphasized the Darwinian nature of strategy, which is composed both of plans for the future and of patterns from the past. These are not always consciously realized and determined, but may be inspired by outside circumstances, people in organizations and leadership. To put it in a nutshell, Mintzberg advocates a voluntaristic approach to the subject of strategy without necessarily rejecting the value of analysis.

At the same time David Hussey in England has stressed the importance of securing acceptance of strategy in a process of organization development. This is rightly emphasized by David Hussey and many others too, but in practice it is more honoured in the breach than in the observance. Co-existence between analysts and behavioural scientists, or determinists and voluntarists to use other terms, is exceedingly hard to bring about.

Now, at the beginning of the 1990s, strategy has had to stand aside and make room for operative skills. Strategy, meaning long-term thinking and vision, has had to give way to short-term improvement of results. Anyone can today understand the reasons for this: companies are in trouble, we are experiencing a profound recession, and the revolutionary structural changes in progress in many countries reinforce the atmosphere of crisis. The victory of market economy over planned economy is not only an East European phenomenon; it is also affecting the planned economy systems that exist in the West within both public and private sectors. Methods like benchmarking and make-or-buy analysis have come into increasing use in both companies and organizations.

Businessmanship

Businessmanship is in fact a mixture of characteristics:

1 The ability to see structural possibilities and to erect better structures by buying and selling companies or business units.
2 The ability to empathize with the need structures of the market and thus satisfy them better than anybody has done before.
3 Skill in managing functional parts of companies to maximize both customer utility and inward efficiency.
4 Leadership in the sense of being able to point out a course and energize people and organizations to follow it.
5 The ability and will to compete by creating competitive advantages at the intersection between customer utility functions and price.

The same thing applies in fields of endeavour other than business. 'Was Adolf Hitler a good leader?' That question can be answered in several ways, but the interesting thing is the way the question itself highlights the difference between the ability to win over people and organizations and the ability to choose a course or strategy. Hitler's chosen strategy was a resounding success in the short term, up to about 1942; in the medium term it was disastrous; in the long term, history records that West Germany emerged as one of the world's 'winner' nations. The question thus illustrates the far-from-clear relationship between leadership ability, strategic ability and time frame.

Leadership is a composite of numerous qualities, many of them of a subtle nature. Businessmanship and leadership are by no means the same thing, though they have some characteristics in common. One often encounters gifted businessmen who lack the leader's talent for inspiring people and are therefore incapable of building up an organization around their business ability.

Customer utility and resource management

The competent modern businessman understands his customers' utility functions and is also skilled in management of resources. Traditional strategy development is based on the Experience Curve relationship between long production runs and low unit costs. In aircraft production before and during World War II it was discovered that unit costs fell by 20 per cent every time the accumulated number of units produced doubled. Applied to large-scale flows, the Experience Curve came to assume a decisive role in strategic thinking right up to the mid-1970s. This was hardly surprising, because demand constantly exceeded supply, which made resource management the key to management success. Just as in the planned economies, productivity was a key issue. As a result of permanent excess demand in many industries, the question of customer utility took second place to rational production over a period of decades.

The new businessman is capable of weighing customer-perceived value against capital and cost management with what has been called holistic vision. These concepts, and the interaction between them, are therefore dealt with extensively under the headings RESOURCES and VALUE in the glossary. We find for example that rational production often comes into conflict with customer-perceived value. Mass production of cars with standardized components lowers their perceived value, as General Motors discovered to its cost in the early 1980s. Using larger aircraft on passenger routes reduces the frequency of service and the number of non-stop flights, which also reduces customer-perceived value.

Those are only a couple of many examples of the conflict between economies of scale and advantages from the customer's point of view. Businessmanship is a matter of resolving such conflicts to the satisfaction of all concerned.

Most functional departments of commercial organizations operate in the conditions of a planned economy. The users of their services do not have a choice of suppliers, which makes their efficiency difficult to judge. The wave of decentralization in the 1980s created a need for businessmanship not only in business units, but also in their functional parts. Techniques such as benchmarking and make-or-buy analysis are now being more widely used to analyze efficiency. (For more on this subject, see COSTS AND CAPITAL, RATIONALIZATION, RESOURCES and VALUE in the glossary.)

Administration, development and entrepreneurship

Modern businessmanship combines management of resources (which involves pruning capital and costs where necessary) with an offensive drive to increase the volume of business through new products and/ or new markets. Traditional business administration generally aims at eliminating risk, which is the safest thing to do in the short and medium term. In the longer term, however, this policy is disastrous, because it involves constantly reducing the scope of business.

Business development has come to mean not just reducing the volume of operations to improve profits, but also establishing a strategic perspective to give a vision of growth. One of the advantages of this kind of behaviour is that it avoids creating a sense of gloom in the organization during the initial phase of the process of change. If you simply announce your intention to cut back on resources (costs and capital), you are apt to generate pessimism that will be an obstacle to making changes. The best people are likely to leave the organization and look for work with other companies. Another important effect of establishing a strategic perspective is that you can start at an early stage to adjust your resources to envisioned future conditions. You do not have to use a scythe to cut down the resource mass, but can concentrate costs and capital in those areas which are expected to be important in the future.

The Austrian economist Joseph Schumpeter spoke of static efficiency as opposed to dynamic efficiency. He was probably referring to the experience of most students attending schools of business administration and the like. They are taught all about cost-revenue analyses, marketing, accounting, administration, finance, etc., and are then assumed to know how to run a business. This assumption has little to support it. People who start businesses seldom have much help from their formal education. We can likewise note the absence of covariation between business entrepreneurship and basic education. Economists display no greater aptitude for or skill in business than do people with other kinds of training. The world is full of non-economists who have proved to be brilliant businessmen.

Parallel to the changes that have swept and are sweeping over Europe, there is an ongoing shift towards more performance-oriented management. This puts dynamic efficiency to the fore, in so far as requirements have expanded to include business development, and not just competent administration of the status quo. I am not casting aspersions on static efficiency, but simply emphasizing the need for dynamic drive in addition to it.

Deregulation and decentralization demand a much greater fund of knowledge

Deregulation has meant that many organizations which once were shielded from competition must now face it head-on. The cost position of European airlines is extremely bad compared to their American counterparts. British Airways have done best, but still have a way to go. Western Europe's telecommunications services are now being deregulated by European Community decree. Their efficiency is far below that of America's Baby Bells. Power generation and distribution are being deregulated, together with monopoly postal services, concurrently with the automatic deregulation arising out of technological development. The inefficiency of farm production in many countries is no longer economically acceptable.

All the people now employed in regulated systems will gradually have to learn the rules of the business strategy game. They must learn how to assess their own efficiency, both operative and strategic. They must learn the terminology and analytical methodology of progressive change. In addition, the situation calls for higher productivity, i.e. more units produced per ecu's worth of resources expended. This is of course a formidable task, which we must all help to try and solve. This book is offered as a contribution to that effort.

In my experience, most managements *assume* business knowledge on the part of many people who do not possess it. They take it for granted that people understand the meaning of terms like corporate mission, balance sheet or strategy without having bothered to teach them the meanings. An overwhelming majority of people in regulated systems have never been exposed to education in businessmanship.

A different situation is presented by the ongoing process of decentralization in many industries and companies. The primary reason why companies decentralize their operations is not to motivate their employees, but because of the stark fact that decentralized systems are much more competitive. Under pressure of competition, it is most efficient to have decisions made as close to the customer as possible. This is what has prompted the move towards more decentralization.

However, organizations are often decentralized without managers and other personnel being supplied with the knowledge of business that they need to take maximum advantage of the competitive potential of decentralization. This is quite unnecessary; it probably happens for the reason mentioned earlier, namely that top management takes it for granted that people are educated, or will educate themselves, in the theory and terminology of business strategy.

Both the situations described above, deregulation and decentralization, call for a balance between structure and dynamics, or between thought and action. Attitudes to this dichotomy tend to be heavily influenced by the current situation. During the 1980s there was no percentage in being analytical, conservative and cautious. Those same characteristics are prized in the early 1990s, while decisiveness and willingness to take risks are no longer so highly esteemed.

Analysis has now come to the fore again because widespread decentralization of companies and other organizations has created a need for strategic ability on the part of a much greater number of individuals. A lot of people are now being trained in strategic thinking, which enhances the efficiency of organizations. At the same time it is increasingly rare for people to be furnished with the analytical tools they need to maximize the effect of strategic ability. For it is just as dangerous to get bogged down in analysis as to disregard the need for strategic analysis. It is therefore high time to strike a blow for analysis, provided that it exists in symbiosis with action. (See further under BUSINESS DEVELOPMENT, CREATIVITY, CULTURE, DIVERSIFICATION, ENTREPRENEURSHIP, NEEDS and VALUES.)

Thus any organization that wants to take maximum advantage of the changed situation created by deregulation and decentralization, with business responsibility devolved to a large number of employees, should make the marginal extra effort represented by proper education in business practice.

Market economy versus planned economy

The above heading may seem somewhat hard, but it was written to underline the contrast between traditional technocratic self-sufficiency and the modern entrepreneurial view. To be satirical, we can say that the technocratic philosophy is based on a sense of one's own superiority and often leads to the belief that one can do everything unaided: 'Why should we let somebody else make component Y for us when we can do it so much better ourselves?'

Some companies have become famous for their pursuit of the ideal of 'vertical integration', i.e. their desire to manufacture as much as possible of their end product in-house rather than buy from subcontractors. A classic case is that of the Singer company, which manufactured every part of its sewing-machines. They owned not only the carpentry shops that made the wooden baseplates for the machines, but also the sawmills that supplied the carpenters with boards and the forests that supplied the sawmills with logs. We have an example in Sweden too. Nordstjernan, whose core business was shipping, integrated forward to importation of coal and backward to manufacture of hull plating steel – and stainless steel too, to make tanks for chemical carriers.

The current trend is for industries to fission into sub-industries. Instead of building a whole car, companies now buy gearboxes, final drives and engines from independent manufacturers, thus giving birth to new industries. Civil aviation is likewise fissioning, farming out engine maintenance and other operations to external contractors. One example is SAS Service Partner, formerly an in-house function of Scandinavian Airline Systems but now a supplier of in-flight meals to many other airlines.

The paradox is that large corporations tend to think like socialist governments. The planning economist's dream is of a totally vertically integrated system that produces everything from iron ore to cars and refrigerators. Big corporations tend to want to make everything that goes into the end product themselves. This pattern is now breaking up to an ever-increasing extent, and to the advantage of all parties concerned including the end user.

Abandoning internal transactions in favour of market transactions promotes keener specialization, more intensive R&D and more rational production. In practice, it means that the buyer has several suppliers to choose from and is not compelled to buy from one (in-house) source. Just as market economies have proved their superiority to planned economies, so is buying and selling between independent companies more efficient than advanced vertical integration. (See further under ORGANIC GROWTH, PRODUCTIVITY/EFFICIENCY AND VERTICAL INTEGRATION in the glossary.)

Economics and business

It was long supposed that the study of economics, specifically of the branch of economics called business administration, endowed the student with enhanced business skills. It has gradually become clear that economics is primarily concerned with management of resources, whereas business looks beyond resources and concentrates on creation of utility for customers as well as rational management.

In the nineteenth century, when Capital held the whip hand over Labour, capitalists often abused their position by exploiting the workers and squeezing wages and conditions to the minimum. Child labour and other such excesses were, dispassionately considered, examples of 'rational management of resources' that offered opportunities for producing goods as cheaply as possible. We of the twentieth century recoil in disgust from such practices. Somewhere, in our minds, there is a dividing line between rational deployment of capital and human resources, and inhuman exploitation.

But what do we know of how posterity, maybe a hundred years from now, will view our behaviour towards workers, office staffs and executives? Stress and pressure to perform may then be regarded as inhuman behaviour, unthinkable to civilized people. Work done by men and women today may be judged as fit only for robots and computers.

Values change, but the fact remains that business practice became suspect and earned a bad reputation during the robber-baron era around the turn of the twentieth century when labour was unscrupulously exploited. That was when Karl Marx, extrapolating from the current behaviour of capitalists, made far-reaching prophesies about the development of society. People today can readily sympathize with the ideals that inspired Marx and other deeply humanistic thinkers then.

During the age of technocracy business practice, in the sense of utility creation combined with administration of resources, gave way to corporate management. The focus was on things that could be analyzed by deduction, and in times when demand outstripped supply, rational management of resources was the prime consideration. With the rise of sales resistance in the mid-1970s the businessman once more gained the upper hand. Empathy and insight into customers' need structures have proved to be indispensable components of successful business management.

Thus the emphasis has shifted from economic skills and techniques to business skills embracing a combination of value creation and resource management. (See further under CORPORATE MISSION, CUSTOMERS, QUALITY and VALUE in the glossary.)

Strategic planning and strategic management

In the technocratic corporate cultures that formerly prevailed, the predominant style of management proceeded from decision-making and control. Strategy was focused on periodical leaps in radically new directions, which absorbed the energies of top management specialists and their supporting staffs. Strategy was often based on forecasts that gave a picture of future developments which in turn led to the formulation of goals in economic terms. The sequence of strategy, then, was:

1 Goals.
2 Strategies, i.e. methods of reaching the goals.
3 Means.

As a consequence of this logic, strategy became the exclusive province of top management. The aim was often to move forward in powerful, distinct steps which were preceded by much crystal ball gazing and intellectual effort, especially on the part of planning staffs and consultants. Generations of MBAs all over the world have been indoctrinated in this logic of strategy.

As the American writer on strategy Robert H. Hayes put it, strategy became more of a map showing the way to the goal than a compass course showing how to navigate in situations of great uncertainty. Strategy as it was practised in those days was naturally a reflection of the apparent predictability of events. Let me here quote Mr Hayes directly:

> Since I began to study American industry almost 30 years ago, there has been a revolution in the science and practice of management, and especially in the attraction of bright, professionally trained managers to the work of strategic planning. Yet as corporate staffs have flourished, and as the notion of strategy has come to dominate business education and practice, our factories have steadily lost ground to those in countries where strategy receives far less emphasis and the 'professionalization' of management is far less advanced.
>
> (Hayes 1985: 111)

Modern strategy proceeds from the enterprise of the many. Knowledge of business conditions in the industry concerned and of the company's corporate mission generates a lush flora of ideas for development within the organization. These ideas prompt choices of course (strategies) which lead the organization into a train of development that generates an economic surplus. Thus strategic thinking spreads throughout the organization, which is a much more efficient set-up in rapidly changing times when the predictability of events is low.

Strategic leadership has come to mean abandoning the strategic plan as a tool of strategy. In fact such a plan is regarded as an obstacle to strategic thinking because it binds the organization to decisions made at top level instead of giving its members a chance to use their own initiative. The strategic plan puts a premium on 'button counters', the people who measure goal fulfilment. Strategic leadership, by contrast, encourages the 'doers', the ones who take the initiative in deed as well as thought. Many of us, when we speak of strategic leadership as opposed to strategic planning, use the distinction to emphasize the difference between the entrepreneurial approach and that of the traditional technocrat. This is one of the chief reasons why the skill capital of companies has acquired such crucial importance in modern business history.

Nearly all large organizations accumulate resources which are in fact irrelevant to the conduct of their business operations. Just as public administrations inevitably grow bureaucratic, it seems equally inevitable that inefficiency in the form of non-essential costs creeps into companies, especially big ones. The public sector is characterized by weak interaction between what is needed and what is done. The feedback system is extremely diffuse, which makes the build-up of resources difficult to control. The organization does not know what resources it really needs, or how strong and frequent the needs are that it is expected to satisfy. Characteristically, in such situations, leaders measure success not by revenues from a market but by the number of employees or the volume of resources (costs and capital) which they control. This generates an urge to empire-building which bears no relation to need. The same thing happens in almost all companies, but the percentage tends to vary directly with the size of the organization.

Non-business resources

An essential part of business development is to try to identify 'non-business resources', meaning costs or capital that do not support business strategies. There may be central departments performing functions that could better be bought from outside. There may also be capital in the form of property, works of art or other 'deadwood' acquired during periods of extreme affluence.

Companies, just like individuals, tend to accumulate a growing volume of bric-à-brac. This is all very well as long as they can afford to support a superstructure of non-business resources, but one may ask whether this surplus value could not be put to more businesslike uses. The managements of technocratic organizations tend to 'put money in the bank', i.e. to consolidate operations and save the surplus.

Deterministic origins of strategy

An important discovery in connection with leadership is the voluntaristic aspect, which means that people can, regardless of circumstances, work wonders if they possess the right motivation and energy.

Strategy originated in a deterministic tradition which holds that possibilities are constrained by circumstances and that there is actually no such thing as free will.

The word voluntarism is derived from the Latin *voluntas*, which means will. Realization of the importance of the individual has expressed itself in many ways, for example through interest in 'human resource management' and the know-how element in all forms of progressive enterprise. 'People are our most important resource' has become one of those clichés that are banal expressions of profound and fundamental truths. The fact is that significant improvements in the productivity of an organization can often be achieved by more efficient utilization of human resources.

Enterprises that develop over a period of time reflect the influence of leaders at different phases of their history. When a new venture is started, and during the initial phase of expansion, it is easy to arouse enthusiasm and energy that lead on to success. Individuals with broad-spectrum business ability then often apply their skills to developing other businesses too, which leads to diversification (*q.v.*).

Diversification requires knowledge of the logics under which different industries operate. When the founder and pioneer leaves the scene, he is often succeeded by a more technocratic type of leader who manages by key economic indicators. People who have business experience, and are capable of understanding the logics of numerous industries, are few and far between.

A common subsequent pattern of development is that technocratic chief executives recruit people like themselves as heads of subsidiaries, which often heralds the start of a period of decline among the latter. This frequently leads to the technocratic management being ousted by a more entrepreneurial management which, under the war-cry of 'back to basics', sells off peripheral companies in the diversified structure. This gradually leads to restored profitability. Eventually the cash surplus grows so large that the company either transforms itself into a holding company for a share portfolio, dabbles in finance, or starts to diversify once more.

This sequence of events has been repeated time and again. Note the parts played by different people at different stages of the sequence. Strategy is only one part of the pattern.

Woo the customer or beat the competitor?

Corporate executives who are games theory buffs tend to view business management primarily as a battle with their competitors. Competitively inclined people naturally want to prove themselves better than those whom they see as their rivals. The question is, however, whether fighting the competition is an efficient focus of effort. Wooing customers is probably much more efficient, because it has the spin-off effect of being a powerful way to compete. Who ever started a company just to do battle with other companies?

Like a climber who tries to get up the career ladder by taking advantage of and trampling on others, the games-theory type of corporate executive measures his success by putting one over on his competitors. The alternative to being a climber is to be competent and diligent, thereby earning the admiration of one's fellows. A businessman, by serving his customers well, can likewise show them that he is more deserving of their custom than his competitors are.

Just as the climber directs his energies to besting those who are competing with him for career advancement, so do some corporate executives direct theirs against their competitors instead of toward their customers. It is of course necessary to take reasonable and reasoned action with regard to competition, but that should never be the main thrust of business except in very special circumstances. (See further under CUSTOMERS, GOALS AND VISION, MARKET and MOTIVATION in the glossary.)

Structure, strategy and operations

Businessmanship can manifest itself in different ways. Businessmen possess varying degrees of aptitude for three distinct aspects of business practice.

Structural issues (portfolio strategy) have to do with the buying and selling of companies or business units in order to achieve more efficient groupings and to earn money from structure-building *per se*. People with such talents range from corporate raiders to less flamboyant commercial empire builders capable of perceiving structural solutions that can be achieved by bold action. Such action often involves a great deal of money and a great deal of confidence in the people who manage the structuring. Sometimes structural manipulation is an expression of corporate strategy, as in the case of Electrolux or United Airlines. In other cases structural change is the name of the game, with dealing and shuffling of combinations of companies as an end in itself.

Business strategy aims at achieving a competitive advantage by combining resources in coherent patterns. This is a kind of businessmanship based primarily on competition with other companies. The aim is not so much to beat the competition as to find competitive advantages, i.e. better ways of satisfying customers' needs and thus gain preference in customers' eyes.

There is no sharp boundary between structural and business strategy. The examples of Electrolux, Volvo Truck and Asea show that structural skill often goes hand in hand with skill in business strategy. Such, however, is not always the case, and it is fair to say that a couple of the aforementioned examples reflect more skill at building structures than in running a competitive business.

Operative ability is a third type of aptitude that characterizes certain businessmen. It generally manifests itself in successful management of resources. This type of businessman has an uncommon ability to identify and eliminate unproductive resources in the form of costs or capital. Here again, operative ability is not the sole explanation of success. It is however a fact that new managements have been able to detect the mistakes of their predecessors in the area of efficient utilization of resources.

It was noted for example by outsiders and reputable consultant firms that the cost level of the Boliden mining group was too high in relation to the average prices of metals over a total market cycle. Since it was difficult to do anything about supply, with respect to either sales volume or prices, the only remaining option was to make a detailed scrutiny of cost and capital structures, and that is what was done. Construction firms and many other companies have likewise been restored to profitability, largely thanks to the application of operative skills.

The foregoing division of business ability into three parts does not claim to be clear-cut; the parts are not mutually exclusive. It can however serve as an aid to analysis of your own set of skills and those of the people around you. (See further under ACQUISITION and FUNCTIONAL/OPERATIVE STRATEGY in the glossary.)

History of business practice

Economic analysis in its original form, based on observations from everyday life, took business more or less for granted. The businessman was a familiar figure from time immemorial, and did not require any particular thought or explanation.

Every social environment brings forth a certain type of business represented by the artisan, the merchant, the moneylender, and so on. No real attempt at a synthetic description of these types was made until near the end of the seventeenth century, when a certain amount of tentative theorization began to appear. Even earlier, however, scholars had drawn a distinction between labour and commerce. That distinction can be traced back to the fifteenth century.

Richard Cantillon, a banker and writer in early eighteenth century Paris, was the first to describe business systematically, and it was he who coined the term *entrepreneur*. Cantillon defined an entrepreneur as one who purchased the means of production at known prices in order to combine them into a product which he hoped to sell for an as yet unknown price. He is committed to his costs, but his profit is uncertain. Cantillon thus recognized business activity as a distinct function in society, pointing out the speculative element that always exists in commerce. This, like most of Cantillon's ideas, was further developed by the Physiocrats, and his teachings became widely known in France.

The French economist Jean Baptiste Say, who lived at the end of the eighteenth century, can be said to have carried on the French tradition by developing the analysis further. Say had first-hand experience in business, and therefore displayed an empathy with the phenomenon of business which other classical economists lacked. To Say, the entrepreneur was one who combined different values into a productive unit. He put the entrepreneur at the centre of both the process of production and the theory of distribution, which was later to influence many other economic theorists.

The Scottish philosopher-economist Adam Smith was strongly influenced by Cantillon and the Physiocrats. He speaks much of 'the master, the merchant and the undertaker' (the last-named in the general sense of one who undertakes something, not in the modern meaning of a mortician). On the other hand he says nothing about the businessman, who plays an astonishingly small part in his analysis of the economic process. One almost gets the impression that he thought this process started and continued spontaneously.

Adam Smith tended to overemphasize the role of labour and to underrate the totality of business within which labour is performed. He further tended to equate capital owners with businessmen. Like many other theorists, he believed that business arose spontaneously in the presence of capital, a labour force and available raw materials.

Entrepreneur and capitalist

In the latter part of the nineteenth century it grew increasingly apparent that a distinction needed to be made between the entrepreneur and the capitalist. New methods of corporate finance led to the creation of a growing number of companies in which the entrepreneurs were not capitalists and the capitalists were not entrepreneurs.

The owner and leader naturally formed the dominant constellation, but it became increasingly clear that no automatic correlation existed. More and more economists began to distinguish between entrepreneurs and capitalists. However, they got themselves into intellectual difficulties because the capitalist is the person who runs the risk, which the entrepreneur does not. Theorization was therefore confused, even though Walker in the United States, Marshall in England and Mangold et al. in Germany placed increasing emphasis on the importance of entrepreneurship.

The distinction between administration and co-ordination of resources on the one hand and creative development of resources on the other was emphatically made by Professor Joseph Schumpeter. He worked in Austria, Germany and the United States in the early part of the twentieth century and strongly influenced later thinkers, despite the fact that the recorded trend in big business was towards increasing technocratization, i.e. administration of the status quo. Schumpeter made an important distinction between adaptive behaviour relative to given resources and creative behaviour under given conditions. In his book *Capitalism, Socialism and Democracy* (1947) he coined the term 'creative destruction'.

Schumpeter used this term to denote the mutability, i.e. the dynamic nature, of economic phenomena, maintaining that clinging to existing thought and structures blocks receptivity to new ideas. He thus strove to emphasize change as an essential ingredient of success in industry and other business activities. If an individual invents a new business combination that fills a need better than existing business combinations, this leads, according to Schumpeter's dynamic theory, to the creative destruction of old structures until something new happens to change the situation.

Schumpeter formulated his basic ideas as early as 1912, but the academic ground for such seeds of thought remained exceptionally stony for more than fifty years. This was because they lacked the mathematical framework that was the pass-key to acceptance in the technocratic era. The ability of the entrepreneur to generate new business solutions at the micro-level was unpredictable and had no place in the structures that scholars needed to work with.

During his lifetime, Schumpeter saw the institutionalization of research and development in big corporations that grew ever bigger and stronger. At the beginning of the 1940s he predicted that development would be dominated by economies of scale and that the entrepreneur would be squeezed out. This extrapolation led, of course, to the conclusion that ultimately there would be only one company left in each industry. Thus Schumpeter grew ever more pessimistic as events in the world around him seemed to refute his theories.

Businessman and administrator

Dr Gunnar Eliasson of IUI in Stockholm has said:

> No progress can be made without mistakes. The technique of society organized on the basis of private capital is to set up a system of rewards to encourage small-scale experimentation to such a degree that many successful projects see the light of day.

A centrally organized society cannot cope with mistakes. The culture of such a society does not readily tolerate mistakes because all major decisions must be made centrally in full awareness that mistakes are not acceptable in theory. This is an extremely inhibitory environment, and the mistakes that are made are large and complicated ones.

Who is to blame for the crisis of the 1970s: Gunnar Sträng (then Sweden's Minister of Finance), Richard Nixon, Lord Keynes or Karl Marx?

Similarly, companies in capitalist-organized societies are specialists in making discoveries, trying things out and taking chances, but also in quickly discovering and correcting mistakes. It is easy to make comparisons to the detriment of public-sector production, which is protected by monopoly legislation and where employees and management can get away with a high degree of incompetence and slackness before market forces catch up with them and force them to change their ways.

The culture and framework of rules that have grown up in the public sector make it difficult or impossible to shut up shop if it turns out that the idea of the business was wrong. How can you shut down the National Labour Market Board or, to be realistic, a State-subsidized company? That is why trial-and-error experimentation is impossible at central State level. We have no effective means of getting rid of something which does not work and which we do not wish to keep.

Several attempts have in fact been made by the public sector to compare input of resources with customer-perceived value. The best-known example is the cost-benefit analysis that was developed during the late 1960s. The trouble is that the results of such an analysis never have any real impact, so the impulse for change is never so strong after an analysis, no matter how good the idea was.

Schumpeter, to recapitulate, spoke of static as opposed to dynamic efficiency. His concept of static efficiency coincides with what I and many others call business administration. It means skill in exploiting a given business situation and managing those parts of a company that are not development-oriented. By dynamic efficiency Schumpeter meant the very driving force that is essential to any process of business development. The thing that depressed Schumpeter was his observation, during the 1920s and 1930s, that things seemed to be prospering by virtue of static efficiency alone. Efficient administration of flows was apparently the key to success. Only much later was it to be tried in the balance and found wanting.

Table 2 Lines of development in business enterprise: an attempt to outline ideological influences on business

	1700	1800	1900	1930	1980	1990
Economics (macro)	**Adam Smith** **D. Ricardo** Value theory; Wage theory; **Cantillon, J. P. Say** 'Entrepreneur'	**J. S. Mill** Induction; Political economy; **K. Marx** Profit; Added value	**J. Schumpeter** Creative destruction; Dynamic efficiency	**J. M. Keynes** Employment: Central planning; Taxation; **D. MacClelland** Performance motivation; Entrepreneurship	1 Crisis of economics 2 Supply-side economics 3 Schumpeter's microworld rehabilitated; **P. Drucker** Innovation; Decentralization; **M. Porter, Kotler, H. Mintzberg** Competition; Dynamics, actors; Customer-perceived value	**O. Williamson** **W. Ouchi** Transaction costs
Businessmanship (micro)			**Ackoff** Operations analysis; Logistics; Planning	**Simon-Mareh** Party model; Decisions; Programmes; **J. Ansoff** Strategic planning; Synergy; Conglomerates; Rational use of resources	**Churchman, Rehman, etc.** Systems theory; Organization as interactive system	**Businessmanship** Resource management, capital and costs; Creation of value
Science, mathematics logistics	**K. von Clausewitz** War planning; War and politics	**F. Taylor, Fayol** Scientific management; Control, instruction; Work specialization; Bureaucracy; Functional organization	**N. Wiener** Cybernetics; Machine man			
Humanities, psychology			**E. Mayo** Human relations; **A. Maslow, F. Herzberg** Motivation; Interest; Involvement		**E. Schein** **Blanchard** **Hersey** Organizational development; Individual and group	Leadership, human resources; Drive and motivation

Schumpeter's story demonstrates that the new business philosophy is not really new at all, and how long it can take before new ideas take root, especially when they are handicapped by a lack of received structure and terminology.

Table 3 The continuum of management

Approximate year	*Individual or ethnic group*	*Major managerial contributions*
5000 BC	Sumerians	script; record keeping
4000	Egyptians	recognized need for planning, organizing, and controlling
2700	Egyptians	recognized need for honesty or fair play in management; therapy interview – 'get it off your chest'
2600	Egyptians	decentralization in organization
2000	Egyptians	recognized need for written word in requests; use of staff advice
1800	Hammurabi	use of witnesses and writing for control; establishment of minimum wage; recognition that responsibility cannot be shifted
1600	Egyptians	centralization in organization
1491	Hebrews	concepts of organization, scalar principle, exception principle
1100	Chinese	recognized need for organization, planning, directing, and controlling
600	Nebuchadnezzar	production control and wage incentives
500	Mencius	recognized need for systems and standards
	Chinese	principle of specialization recognized
	Sun Tzu	recognized need for planning, directing, and organizing
400	Socrates	enunciation of universality of management
400	Xenophon	recognized management as a separate art
	Cyprus	recognized need for human relations; use of motion study, layout, and materials handling
350	Greeks	scientific method applied; use of work methods and tempo
	Plato	principle of specialization enunciated
325	Alexander the Great	use of staff
175	Cato	use of job descriptions
50	Varro	use of job specifications
20 AD	Jesus Christ	unity of command; golden rule; human relations
284	Diocletian	delegation of authority

Approximate year	Individual or ethnic group	Major managerial contributions
900 AD	Alfarabi	listed traits of a leader
1100	Ghazali	listed traits of a manager
1340	L. Paccioli (Genoese)	double-entry bookkeeping
1395	Francisco Di Marco	cost accounting practised
1410	Soranzo Brothers	use of journal entries and ledger
1418	Barbarigo	forms of business organization; work in process accounts used
1436	Arsenal of Venice Venetians	cost accounting; checks and balances for control; numbering of inventoried parts; interchangeability of parts; use of assembly line technique; use of personnel management; standardization of parts; inventory control; cost control
1500	Sir Thomas More	called for specialization; decried sins of poor management and leadership
1525	Niccolo Machiavelli	reliance on mass consent principle; recognized need for cohesiveness in organization; enunciated leadership qualities
1767	Sir James Steuart	source of authority theory; impact of automation
1776	Adam Smith	application of principle of specialization to manufacturing workers; control concepts; payback computations
1785	Thomas Jefferson	called attention to concept of interchangeable parts
1799	Eli Whitney	scientific method; use of cost accounting and quality control; applied interchangeable parts concept; recognized span of management
1800	Jarnes Watt Matthew Boulton Soho, England	standard operating procedures; specifications; work methods; planning; incentive wages; standard times; standard data; employee Christmas parties; bonuses announced at Christmas; mutual employees' insurance society; use of audits
1810	Robert Owen New Lanark, Scotland	need for personnel practices recognized and applied; assumed responsibility for training workers; built clean terraced homes for workers
1820	James Mill	analyzing and synthesizing human motions
1832	Charles Babbage	scientific approach emphasized; specialization emphasized; division of labour; motion and time study; cost acounting; effect of various colours on employee efficiency

Approximate year	Individual or ethnic group	Major managerial contributions
1835 AD	Marshall, Laughlin, et al.	recognition and discussion of the relative importance of the functions of management
1850	Mill et al.	span of control; unity of command; control of labour and materials; specialization – division of labour; wage incentives
1855	Henry Poor	principles of organization, communication, and information applied to railways
1856	Daniel C. McCallum	use of organization chart to show management structure; application of systematic management to railways
1871	W. S. Jevons	made motion study of spade use; studied effect of different tools on worker; fatigue study
1881	Joseph Wharton	established college course in business management
1886	Henry C. Metcalfe	art of management; science of administration
	Henry R. Towne	science of management
1891	Frederick Halsey	premium plan of wage payment
1900	Frederick W. Taylor	scientific management; systems applications; personnel management; need for co-operation between labour and management; high wages; equal division between labour and management; functional organization; exception principle applied to the shop; cost system; methods study; time study; definition of scientific management; emphasis on management's job; emphasis on research standards, planning, control, and co-operation
	Frank B. Gilbreth	science of motion study; therbligs
1901	Henry L. Gantt	task and bonus system; humanistic approach to labour; Gantt charts; management's responsibility for training workers
1910	Hugo Munsterberg	application of psychology to management and workers
	Harrington Emerson	efficiency engineering; principles of efficiency
1911	Harlow S. Person	initiated first scientific management conference in United States; gave academic recognition to scientific management
1911	J. C. Duncan	first college text in management

Approximate year	Individual or ethnic group	Major managerial contributions
1915 AD	H. B. Drury	criticism of scientific management – reaffirmed initial ideas
	R. F. Hoxie	criticism of scientific management – reaffirmed initial ideas
	F. W. Harris	economic lot size model
	Thomas A. Edison	devised war game to evade and destroy submarines
1916	Henri Fayol	first complete theory of management; functions of management; principles of management; recognized need for management to be taught in schools
	Alexander H. Church	functional concept of management; first American to explain the totality of managerial concepts and relate each component to the whole
	A. K. Erlang	anticipated waiting-line theory
1917	W. H. Leffingwell	applied scientific management to office
1918	C. C. Parsons	recognized need for applying scientific management to offices
	Ordway Tead	application of psychology to industry
1919	Morris L. Cooke	diverse applications of scientific management
1921	Walter D. Scott	brought psychology to advertising and personnel management
1923	Oliver Sheldon	developed a philosophy of management; principles of management
1924	H. F. Dodge	use of statistical inference and
	H. G. Romig	probability theory in sampling
	W. A. Shewhart	inspection and in quality control by statistical means
1925	Ronald A. Fisher	various modern statistical methods including chi-square test, Bayesian statistics, sampling theory, and design of experiments
1927	Elton Mayo	sociological concept of group endeavour
1928	T. C. Fry	statistical foundations of queuing theory
1930	Mary P. Follett	managerial philosophy based on individual motivations; group process approach to solving managerial problems.
1931	James D. Mooney	principles of organization recognized as universal
1938	Chester Barnard	theory of organization; sociological aspects of management; need for communication
1938	P. M. S. Blackett et al.	operations research

Approximate year	Individual or ethnic group	Major managerial contributions
1943 AD	Lyndall Urwick	collection, consolidation, and correlation of principles of management
1947	Max Weber Rensis Likert Chris Argyris	placed emphasis on psychology, social psychology, and research in human relations in organization theory; incorporation of an open-system theory of organization
1949	Norbert Wiener Claude Shannon	emphasized systems analysis and information theory in management
1951	Frank Abrams Benjamin M. Seleckman	reintroduced managerial statesmanship in managerial thinking
1955	Herbert Simon Harold J. Levitt Robert Schlaifer	placed emphasis on human behaviour in decision-making, viewed as an identifiable, observable, and measurable process; increased attention given to managerial psychology
1960	Douglas McGregor	the attitude of the manager towards his subordinates is a heavy influence on their behaviour and work climate within the organization; theory X stands for controlling manager and theory Y for responsibility allocation
1965	Igor Ansoff	questions early methods of long-range planning and proposes a model for strategic planning (he later on denounces this approach in his book *Strategic Management*, 1979)
1967	Fred Fledler Richard House	continuity theories in leadership dealing with orientation towards tasks and relation respectively
1967	James Thompson Jay Galbraith P. Lawrence J. Lorsche	acknowledgement that there is no universal optimum method of organizing activities, and further inquiries into the situational aspect of organizational design
1969	Karl Weick	studies of organizations as interpreted systems
1975	William Ouchi Oliver Williamson	the development of the theory of firm; deals with imperfections in markets as a reason for the existence of firms
1975	Henry Mintzberg	deals with organizational structures from the machine bureaucracy through *ad hoc*-cracy
1975–1980	Gerald Salancik Geoffrey Pfeffer Michael Crousier	theories on power structures within and between organizations

Approximate year	Individual or ethnic group	Major managerial contributions
1976 AD	Rosemary Stewart	choices and constraints in the managerial world situation; differentiates between various types of managerial tasks
1980	Michael Porter	proposes new theories on competitive strategy dealing with competitive forces, value creation for customers and resources in terms of costs
1982	John Kotter John Gabarro	the dynamics of top executive work; distinct characteristics as perceived over time
1982	Terence Deal Alan Kennedy	create a concept of corporate culture as an important influence on organizational behaviour and corporate development
1985	Tom Peters	dealing with customers as human beings and people in the organization as important resources for business development

Glossary

ACQUISITION

Acquisition is a common growth technique. By buying a business or shares in a company you can grow in quantum jumps, whereas ORGANIC GROWTH is a matter of gradual expansion based on resources the company has generated from its own business operations.

A great deal of research has been done on acquisition as a method of corporate development. It shows that in the great majority of cases the seller is the more satisfied party, while shockingly often the buyer is dissatisfied with his acquisition.

The techniques of acquisition and the process of administering the acquired business have been greatly improved in recent years, so that buyers nowadays generally manage to avoid the most usual traps for the unwary, like extrapolating result curves which are abnormally high due to temporary circumstances. We sometimes hear of soufflé companies whose profit levels are inflated by a process of cost cutting which cannot be sustained in the long run and will eventually damage business. It is possible to hike profits considerably in the short term by stopping expenditure on development of products, people and markets.

Another pitfall connected with acquisition is the buyer's tendency to be in too much of a hurry to remould a going concern to match his own business structure, without paying enough attention to the factors that contributed to success before the acquisition. Apart from sabotaging the acquired company's corporate mission, the buyer risks losing its most capable people, in the worst case to competitors.

We can distinguish three rational motives for acquisition:

1 To fill a gap in a portfolio
2 To invest a surplus
3 To strengthen a business unit

To these three we must add a fourth, which is irrational in terms of business but none the less extremely common, namely the empire-building urge.

If you want to fill a gap in a portfolio, your aim may be to acquire a missing product to satisfy the structure of customer needs in a given area, to utilize the capacity of a distribution channel, or something else. Volvo's acquisition of Daf was originally prompted by the need to strengthen its bargaining position with dealers by adding a smaller and cheaper car to its range. A data consultancy firm that buys up a firm of training specialists obviously plans to satisfy its customer's need for training in the installation and operation of computer systems.

Frank Lorenzo's acquisition of US Airlines seems to have been prompted by a combination of industry restructuring and empire-building.

Investing a surplus is often the underlying motive in boom periods when companies' cash flows take an upturn. Although there are nearly always opportunities for investing in the principal business, consider-ations of risk or timing may make it advisable to put the money into something else.

Closely akin to the cash-investment motive is that of acquiring an apparently badly managed company. You may have had the oppor-tunity to observe how a management has handled its business, and come to the conclusion that you could quickly improve its profits by buying it and putting in new management. Such a situation naturally represents a business opportunity where the investment can pay off handsomely.

The third rational motive for acquisition is to strengthen a business unit. The item acquired may be a competitor, a supplier, a new distri-bution channel or a new technology. Buying out a competitor just to get a bigger market share may be justified in situations where there are tangible economies of scale to be won in distribution or production. In the express package business in the United States, for example, market share is crucial to the frequency of delivery in a given district and thus to a company's ability to make express deliveries at a reason-able cost.

In other cases there are substantial economies to be made through longer production runs. However, the advance of modern technology has made this last case less typical now than it used to be. Economies of scale in production are often overrated as a competitive advantage.

Regardless of its motive for acquisition, the prospective buyer must assess the value of the potential acquiree as a basis for negotiation. Empirical data show that in 80 per cent of all acquisitions, the buyer, two years after the event, considers the acquisition a disappointment, while about the same proportion of sellers are satisfied with the deal they made. In other words, acquisition is a very difficult art as regards both strategic assessment and operative handling.

The mistake most often made by acquirers is to misjudge the strategic position and operational skills of the acquiree. One of the most important things the buyer must do, then, is to judge the strategic attractiveness of the potential acquiree balanced against the latter's operational ability. Table 4 shows how two businesses with the same return on investment can differ very widely in their future profit potential.

Table 4 A comparison of two companies' return on investment

Assessment	Company A	Company B
Return on investment	20%	20%
Market share	small	large
Relative market share	small	large
Relative product quality	low	high
Capital-to-turnover ratio	high	low
Capital per employee	low	high
Added value per employee	average	average
Market growth	low	high
Outlook	Excellent	Disastrous

The fact that companies A and B show the same return on investment may simply be a coincidence, or it may be due to a marked difference in management competence. As in all other business situations, it is necessary to grasp the trade logic under which the acquiree operates in order to make a correct assessment of its present performance.

There is a wealth of literature on the subject giving checklists, screening methods and other techniques applicable to acquisition. In this context I have made a selection of questions of crucial importance:

How much profit is the acquiree expected to generate?

It is becoming common practice to link the purchase price to the growth rate of the acquiree's earnings, so that the seller is made to give a firm undertaking. Expectations of future earnings must of course be weighed against the purchase price, so an assessment of how realistic those expectations are is often a useful check question.

Can a weakness in the acquiree be corrected?

Replacing the management is one possibility already mentioned. In other cases the buyer may have noted weaknesses in marketing organization, production or other functions that can immediately be put right and thereby bring about a quick improvement in profitability.

Will the acquisition complement the present portfolio, and if so how?

Advocates of planned acquisition often argue for synergies which do not in fact exist. Especially where the real motive is empire building, there is a tendency to camouflage that motive by pointing to synergies of a diffuse nature. It is of course perfectly legitimate to make such bogus synergies the cover story for public consumption, as long as you are honest enough with yourself to recognize your true motives.

How much is the acquisition worth?

You can arrive at the answer to this question by proceeding from the top price you are willing to pay in view of the value the acquisition can have to your own company. This kind of reasoning is often very helpful in clarifying the framework of negotiations. Though due deliberation before decision is a virtue as far as acquisitions are concerned, there is seldom much time for it.

The purpose of this entry is to clarify the true motives for acquisition and to offer a few points to ponder and questions to ask. I would like to mention in conclusion that I have known heads of companies who, with very little formal analysis, have made entrepreneurial acquisitions that turned out to be enormously successful. In one instance, a medium-sized acquisition deal was concluded in two days, much to the annoyance of two other companies who had been negotiating with the seller for a couple of months. Knowledge of the technology of acquisition is essential and can save a lot of time.

ACTIVITY-BASED COSTING

Certain circumstances have played a significant part in the emergence of a partly new approach to cost allocation. One important aspect of the background is that the growing complexity of industrial systems has led to a gradual decline in the proportion of direct material and labour costs, with a corresponding and continuing rise in the proportion of joint costs.

In the days when direct materials and labour accounted for the lion's share of the costs of a product, it was acceptable to make a routine allocation of joint costs in proportion to variable separable costs. Latterly, however, this basis for allocation has come to be seen as very unreliable.

The old principles for allocating joint costs seem to have taken root and continue to be used out of sheer laziness, for changes in cost accounting methods involve criticism, reappraisal and all the other uncomfortable things associated with change. The fact of the matter is quite simply that indirect costs have assumed an increasingly dominant role. As a well-known firm of accountants put it, 'There used to be two bookkeepers for every eight smiths. Now there are eight bookkeepers for every two smiths.' The result is that standard products have tended to subsidize special products and services, and that high-volume products subsidize those parts of the range which are produced in smaller quantities.

The diagrams below illustrate the traditional methods, cost price costing and margin contribution costing.

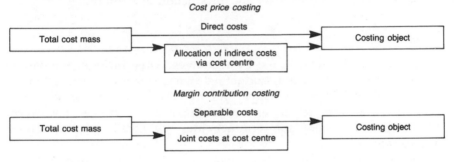

Costing models: Principles of cost price and margin contribution costing

The problem, as we see, is that reality has moved farther and farther away from these models as business has grown more complex. The principle of activity-based accounting, ABC, is similarly illustrated as follows:

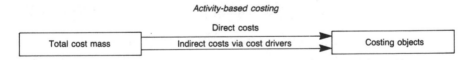

Definition of activity based costing

The following sequence is an important foundation of ABC:

1 Survey usage of resources, activity by activity.
2 Survey activities, revenue bearer by revenue bearer.
3 Relate cost drivers to activities.

This links costs to the objects that give rise to costs. It means that a product or service which is a heavy consumer of resources will be identified as expensive according to ABC.

Four elements need to be defined within the framework of ABC: objects; resources; activities; cost drivers

Objects

Objects are the targets of costing. They are usually products, but may also be customers, markets, groups of products, etc.

Resources

Resources do work and thus generate costs. Examples of resources are personnel, computer systems and production machinery.

Activities

Activities are the work done by resources. They include purchasing of raw materials, invoicing, budgeting, market planning, etc. Activities can be defined in many ways and may be more or less detailed. Although the term resources by definition also includes 'hardware' like factory machinery, the term activities is generally used to denote human activities.

Cost drivers

A cost driver is the quantity that links activities to the object which is the target of the ABC model. The number of works orders can be a cost driver, for example. To be usable, a cost driver must be communicable, controllable and accepted in the organization. Cost drivers used for purposes of costing must also relate to the cost object. This means that a cost driver used for calculating product costs must be relatable to individual products.

The first step in an ABC analysis is to define the cost drivers and their underlying activities. The two can be derived concurrently, and the result will depend largely on how the ABC model is set up with regard to aims, thoroughness and, of course, access to relevant data.

Defining activities is a time-consuming business, and one that calls for close attention to detail. Once activities and objects have been defined, the cost drivers must be established. This requires a substantial investment of man-hours, for ABC is not so much a cost accounting system as an analytical tool to provide input for management decisions. It can suitably be used from time to time in support of decisions that will guide business in the right direction.

Here follows a list of the advantages of ABC:

1 Emphasis on causal cost relationships is valuable in that it prompts careful analysis, which otherwise is seldom made.
2 Activities replace the more traditional cost centres used for division of a company into value-generating units. This can be related to the company's value chain.
3 The two stages have educational value, in that the first identifies the consumption of resources per activity and the second shows how these activities are 'consumed' by revenue bearers, i.e. products and services.
4 Establishing cost drivers leads to a much deeper understanding of the company's efficiency.
5 Known factors such as the Experience Curve, economies of scale, synergies, capacity utilization and quality emerge in a clearer light when viewed in the perspective of ABC.
6 Routine cost allocation with heavy charges on direct material and wage costs is avoided, while all costs are taken into account.
7 Capacity costs are assessed at full utilization, eliminating arbitrary variations.
8 The risk of suboptimization in the organization is detected more efficiently when ABC is used.
9 Large numbers of people are involved in data acquisition. This educates the whole organization.
10 The costs in question can be followed up not only by products or services but also by other objects such as customers or geographical markets.

The very fact that the method is being marketed under a new name, and that it involves so many people in the organization, is valuable in itself. The old cost accounting methods needed reforming, and in this context ABC has helped to release new energy for assessing questions of productivity.

ABC just like any other method, has its pitfalls and traps for the unwary. Let us list some of them – not, let me emphasize, to discourage the use of ABC but simply as a guide to making the most effective use of it.

1 It is easy to place too much emphasis on cost-effectiveness at the expense of competitiveness. Although it is always right to consider productivity, doing things right, you must also consider whether the right things are being done.
2 There is no getting away from the fact that some costs are fixed. Especially in short-term decision situations, it is always permissible to make a rough allocation of fixed joint costs.

3 An ABC analysis can swell to such complexity that the overview is lost. Keys to cost allocation must be related to credible cost drivers, otherwise the method itself will lose credibility.

4 The division of responsibility within the organization with regard to costs is not the same thing as activities, cost drivers and objects. The organizational consequences must not be underestimated.

5 Cost relationships are often variable, non-linear and non-additive. It is easy to underestimate the degree of complexity, which is sometimes an advantage but can also be a disadvantage.

6 There is of course a risk of finding false correlations, so it is important to understand not just the correlation itself but also the causality.

7 Costs for things like R&D and marketing may be viewed either as present costs for maintenance of competitiveness and relative competence *vis-à-vis* customers, or as costs for future products and services.

8 The Experience Curve, advantages of scale and synergies all naturally have a strong influence on productivity. However, to maintain competitiveness it may be necessary to accept short runs and apparent inefficiencies which the market demands and is prepared to pay for.

9 At worst, ABC can lead to 'internal pseudo-commercialization' with complicated and misleading internal pricing.

10 Eventually, in a steady state, ABC could lead to the same kind of routine allocation of costs that cost price costing has done.

ABC has washed over the United States like a wave in recent years. It has been used by the giant General Motors corporation, who have applied it in 50 of their 193 plants in North America. There it has been found that high-volume products incur lower overheads than products manufactured in smaller quantities.

The next step after ABC is ABM, Activity Based Management. This embraces not only activities and cost drivers, but also how activities can be utilized to satisfy customers' utility functions and thus contribute to creation of value.

Awareness of both the advantages and risks of the method makes it much more powerful. Let me therefore warmly recommend ABC, while urging you to remember its limitations and hazards. If you do, ABC can be just the valuable aid to rationalization that it has proved to be in so many cases.

BARRIERS

The word barrier actually means 'an elongated structure erected as an obstacle or shield'. By analogy, the word as used in the context of business strategy refers to the creation of obstacles either to prevent new competition from starting or to prevent existing competitors from leaving the market.

The erection of a barrier is part of the struggle to gain a competitive edge. The nature of the barrier may vary. Traditionally, it is a question of high capital intensity. In the airline business, the barriers consist of concessions and large sums of capital. In many kinds of consultancy business it is know-how that is the barrier. In the retail trade it is the location of the shop or some other competitive advantage that makes it hard for competitors to break in. Barriers of this kind are called entry barriers; some examples are given below.

Entry barriers

- economies of scale: high investment needed to achieve low production costs
- differentiated product: customers loyal to one brand or supplier
- capital requirement: high capital outlay for credit, image or whatever
- changeover costs: cost to customer of changing suppliers
- distribution channels: none available
- components and raw materials: deliveries unobtainable
- location: already occupied
- lack of experience and know-how
- expected retaliation: competitors will gang up on a newcomer
- price cutting
- patents

Exit barriers

In many industries, exit barriers have proved to be a serious obstacle to long-term profitability. The world shipbuilding industry is a classic example. Many nations have built huge shipyards and invested billions of dollars in them. When a situation of overcapacity arises, the investors fight tooth and nail to hold on to their investment, with the result that capacity is not knocked out fast enough to allow anybody to make a profit. The same thing has happened in the steel industry and is probably about to happen in the aviation industry. Examples of exit barriers include:

- write off of heavy investments

- prestige and image
- management pride
- government intervention
- high disengagement costs: restoration of site
- trade union opposition
- shared costs that will have to be borne by another product or market
- suppliers, customers, distributors

The purpose of entry barriers, of course, is to deter new competitors from trying to get established. The idea is to make the cost of admission to the market place so high as to risk a negative return on the capital that must be invested. Entry barriers can thus be designed either to raise the admission fee or to increase the risk to the new-comer.

Exit barriers, on the other hand, force business units to keep on operating in an industry where profitability is low or return on capital is negative. As you can see from the list above, exit barriers can be divided into three classes: socio-political, economic and emotional. The last-named group includes the situation where a successful conglomerate branches out into a new field and stubbornly keeps the venture going year after year despite heavy losses. Such situations are not uncommon, and they can often create serious problems for established companies in the industry concerned.

In most strategic situations it is very important to identify the relevant entry and exit barriers.

Opportunities for competition on advantageous terms are the opposite of barriers. Just as regulation of an industry, for example, constitutes an effective entry barrier, so deregulation creates a situation where competitiveness is put to the test. In such cases the existing operators have often burdened themselves with top-heavy cost and capital structures that they find hard to get rid of; this means that newly established companies can start from a highly advantageous relative cost position.

The airline industry is a good present-day example. Many established airlines are tangled up in costly union agreements and heavy capital investments, e.g. in terminal buildings. In 1992 Scandinavian Airlines System abandoned its newly built domestic terminal at Arlanda Airport in Sweden.

Investments during the epoch of regulation were often made with relatively low precision, and this has given new companies excellent opportunities to break into the market.

BENCHMARKING (BEST PRACTICE STUDIES)

Benchmarking is a term borrowed from surveying, where a benchmark is a fixed point used as a reference for establishing altitudes and locations. In a business context, the term has come to be widely used to mean comparisons of performance between different departments of companies with regard to productivity, i.e. to costs, time and quality. A benchmarking project can appear deceptively simple at first sight. There are however a number of success factors and pitfalls of which one needs to be aware.

If we wish to measure efficiency in an organization, i.e. the function of value and productivity, there is usually a result at overall level that can be taken as a starting point. In a business organization this result can be read from the profit-and-loss account. In organizations of other kinds it may appear from other figures such as membership or market share. Even if the overall result is satisfactory, there may still be considerable room for improvement in various functional parts of the organization. A department within a total organization exists in a planned-economy environment, i.e. in a situation where the recipients of the goods or services which it produces are not free to choose alternative suppliers. This means that the powerful incentives to efficiency inherent in a market economy cannot operate. Benchmarking can be considered, quite simply, as a substitute for the efficiency-promoting effect of market forces.

How to organize a benchmarking project

The sequence of steps in carrying out a benchmarking project is listed below.

1 Secure acceptance of the method.
2 What is to be compared?
3 To whom and what?
4 Establish efficiency gaps.
5 Establish time-related target figures for each department.
6 Communicate results for acceptance.
7 Draw up plans of action.
8 Supervise implementation and provide support for the process.

The purpose of benchmarking is to achieve substantial improvements in the organization and the content of its work. Credibility and formulation of relevant target figures are therefore of decisive importance.

The apparent simplicity of the benchmarking method often results in its being technocratized. Differences in basic activities are ignored and target figures are mechanically set, making the whole exercise counter-productive.

A distinction is usually made between three related but somewhat different types of benchmarking:

1 *Best demonstrated practice* means that the study refers to similar production units within the same organization.
2 *Relative cost position* means that the comparison is made between equivalent functions in different organizations within the same industry.
3 *Best related practice* means comparisons between similar functions in different industries, the object being to search for excellence wherever it may be found.

Consequences of benchmarking

Benchmarking is applied to productivity, i.e. number of units produced in relation to input of resources, as well as to value, i.e. users perception of utility in relation to price. In the accompanying efficiency graph one axis represents value and the other productivity. The benchmarking method can thus be used for both cases, with a number of possible consequences:

1 Higher productivity.
2 Better products.
3 Revised pricing.
4 Greater efficiency.
5 Input for make-or-buy analyses.
6 Quality programmes.
7 Programmes for time-based competition.
8 Adjustments in the organization.

The foregoing list is a mixture of general effects and specific actions. The important thing is to appreciate the contribution that benchmarking can make to efficiency.

BUSINESS DEVELOPMENT

The term business development has come to represent a holistic view of business operations involving consideration of both resource structures and customer-perceived values.

Business development is a special case of strategy, but it has come into use because the term strategy development was formerly applied for the most part to either portfolio strategies or cost and capital rationalization. The term business development refers to:

1 Increasing the volume of business.
2 Directing energy towards customers and markets.
3 Generating new business.
4 Generating creativity and drive in the organization by focusing on customers and their needs.

Business development contributes to increasing the volume of business. It thus includes a series of actions which, unlike cost reduction measures, have the ultimate aim of expanding the company's operations – which must of course remain profitable in the long term. Business development may, however, just like any other forward-looking programme such as an upgrading of quality, have a negative effect on profitability in the short term.

Another aim of business development is to revitalize the existing main business and to increase the radiation of outward-directed energy at the expense of internal energy consumption. I resort to these somewhat grandiose expressions after having observed a number of organizations which, as they grew, began to expend more and more energy on maintaining and preserving the basic organization itself. Internal conferences, reshuffling production apparatus and personnel, a constant growth of internal communications and so on, make it all too easy to forget about customers and to use up more and more energy on inward things. This is one of the main reasons why companies lose their ability to compete. The increasing internal energy consumption is unfortunately accompanied by dwindling alertness to the changing pattern of customers' needs.

Business development can also be defined as increased scope of delivery. This means that customers are encouraged to decide to buy goods and services which were not previously part of the product range. Unfortunately, this kind of expansion is often undertaken without prior analysis of the 'ideal scope of delivery', i.e. of how many buying decisions customers are prepared to make at the same time.

During the carefree 1980s there was a tendency to offer packages, such as travel agency services provided by airlines, which were put together without any analysis of customers' buying behaviour. The world is full of such packages which have proved to be less than optimal in terms of customers' willingness to buy them. Yet it is a comparatively simple exercise to acquire a fact base on this important point. The conclusion is that precision in marketing deteriorated during the boom years of the 1980s.

Traditional strategy strives for efficient utilization of resources in the form of capital and costs. Experience curves and the optimization models developed in the 1950s and 1960s all had that aim. The rationale

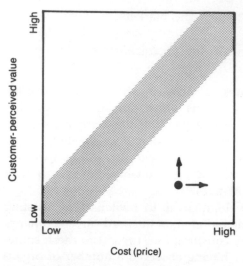

Figure 2 Value graph. Companies should try to place their products in the diagonal zone (shaded), which is where the customer feels he is getting value for his money.

for striving in that direction was that goods were in short supply in most areas, and demand could therefore be taken for granted.

After the cataclysmic events of the mid-1970s, corporate development was perforce extended to embrace the vertical dimension, that is the value variable. This was how the concept of business development came to embrace a holistic view in the sense that all the dimensions of business management had to be included in the work of strategy. The value graph (Figure 2) covers the generation of values, both the tangible, quantifiable kind and the other more subtle kind that cannot be motivated on strictly rational grounds. Those subtle elements exist in all buying situations, even in ostensibly rational buying decisions in an industrial environment.

The trouble is that the creation of values often conflicts with effective utilization of resources. Long production runs and low unit costs are often a rational way to make use of capital equipment, materials and labour, but they reduce the value of the product as the customer perceives it.

Large aircraft are cheaper for airlines to operate per passenger mile, but have the drawback from the traveller's point of view that departures are fewer and further between. A car that is mass-produced with standard engines, colours and so on is cheap to manufacture, but the lack of differentiation detracts from its value in the eyes of the motorist. Similar conflicts occur in many industries, and it is an essential part of businessmanship to balance the components of efficient resource utilization and customer-perceived value against each other.

The traditional view of business in Europe differs from that which prevails in the United States. Ever since the Experience Curve was first described in America in 1926, the emphasis of commercial operations there has been heavily on cost advantages in manufacturing. The large, homogeneous market of the United States, free from regional barriers, has stimulated cost-based, and thus price-based, competition.

In Europe, on the other hand, we have had a jumble of small regional and national markets which has prompted greater interest in quality as a means of competition. Value is the quotient between quality and price, so concentrating on *either* costs *or* business development is not a satisfactory solution. It is thus the task of leadership to balance the parameters according to the situation.

BUSINESSMANSHIP

The old concept of the businessman has been rehabilitated. According to the dictionary it means a person professionally occupied in commerce. In the terminology of modern economics, the word may have the following meaning:

> A businessman is a person with the ability to understand the need structures of customers and to combine that understanding with knowledge of capital and costs in order to create economic value. The businessman can creatively combine needs and production resources, and has the capital, costs and energy to initiate business. The businessman operates in a market economy, i.e. one where customers can choose between different suppliers.

The trouble with businessmanship is that it is not a discipline in the customary academic sense. Some disciplines have been devised to teach functional parts of businessmanship, such as accounting, finance, marketing and distribution. Businessmanship in the twentieth century has been influenced by a number of sciences. Mathematics has become a necessary tool of accounting and cost-revenue analysis. Biology has had a strong influence through cybernetics, as has psychology and, at times, religion and philosophy too. But because of the complex nature of businessmanship, very little research has been done on the subject as a whole.

A somewhat different type of businessmanship is characterized by the ability to perceive structural possibilities. Many financiers buy companies, sell some of their assets or business units, and divide up the remainder in ways that give each business unit a more efficient structure. This has not so much to do with customer-perceived value as with the ability to visualize optimum business structures.

Businessmanship is a commodity in short supply in large corporations and technocratic environments. The demand for businessmen is now growing as a result of the ongoing wave of privatization and shift to market economy in various sectors of society. This has led to the term being used and over-used in a way that sometimes obscures its meaning.

To begin with, businessmanship assumes that the customer, recipient or user of the service has a choice between alternative suppliers. It is the customer's ability to reject alternatives, thereby informing the supplier that he needs to improve his price-performance ratio, that provides the urge to efficiency.

Two things that are often confused are a business transaction and a business relationship. People who lack first-hand business experience sometimes tend to give the term businessmanship a connotation of sharp practice, of maximizing one's own short-term advantage at the other fellow's expense. In one-off business transactions, for example when you sell your bicycle to somebody you will probably never have dealings with again, you can maximize your own short-term advantage. The normal situation, however, is that you build up a business relationship; this means that there must be a clear mutual advantage in doing business, so that both parties are keen for the relationship to continue as it is. It is necessary to understand the difference between a business transaction and a business relationship.

BUSINESS UNIT

A business unit is the fundamental particle for which a business strategy is formulated. A business unit operates with a specific corporate mission in a specific market defined by four basic parameters:

- a defined product comprising goods and/or services
- specified needs to be satisfied
- a group of customers
- a competitive edge

This definition of a business unit implies that some part of a business is demarcated as doing a particular kind of business. When doing this, one should look at the factors and functions that link the business unit to other areas of business.

An industry is, then, the sum of all the business units that exist to supply a given area of need. An industry has nothing to do with formal and legal corporate structures. The reason why I have put business units before industries is that in determining the strategy for

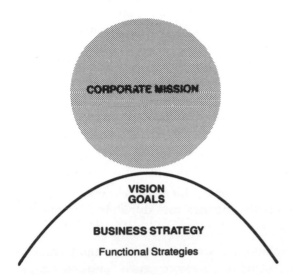

Figure 3 Relation between some important concepts

a business unit you should always make an analysis of the competition in that part of the industry that operates in or near your company's market. A European or American construction company will probably not need to analyse the construction industry in New Zealand.

SAS is an example of a corporation comprising different business units. SAS has two synergistic business units, passenger traffic and air freight. Synergies are the results generated by a group of business units relative to the sum of what their individual results would have been if they had operated independently. In addition, SAS includes business units like Service Partner and hotels. Most of these units have synergies, including one whose corporate mission is to calibrate aircraft compasses.

Another example of a corporation with multiple business units is Volvo: its business structure includes cars, buses, trucks, aero engines, energy, foods and others.

Business units are sometimes referred to by the abbreviation SBU, which stands for Strategic Business Unit. The definition of the term may in appropriate cases need to be supplemented by two important aspects.

Firstly, it may sometimes be necessary to define a relevant group of competitors. These competitors exist on different levels, from producers of substitutes, i.e. of other products that satisfy the same needs, to companies offering identical goods and services.

The second aspect, which is related to the first, has to do with the technological frame of reference. This is sometimes important. Let us take the case of communication, which is a highly topical one. Business communications may take the form of air travel, rail travel, car travel or video conferences. When we think of an airline, we usually think of its competitors as consisting of other airlines, making certain assumptions about the technology of communication. But competition may also come from other areas of technology, in this case telecommunications. Such substitutes (alternative means of satisfying the same need) are generally ignored in the definition of a business unit, though they are often an important strategic consideration.

CHANGE, PROCESS OF

You cannot accomplish a process of business development without thought and action, without both structural and dynamic components. A suggested sequence might be:

1 Decide on your level of ambition, analyse the business and formulate your portfolio mission, corporate mission, goals and strategies. There are many methods, models and procedures for doing this. Structures that are too rigid can be constricting. Document the converging part of the strategy development process.

2 Develop a management philosophy setting forth the guiding corporate values of the organization as a whole. This management philosophy must be documented.

3 Set up an organization compatible with your corporate mission, goals and strategies. The organization must be business-oriented; keep supporting functions to a minimum. The organization must cover:
   – philosophy;
   – theoretical principles of structure;
   – definition of responsibilities;
   – interactive roles;
   – demarcation between units;
   – instruments for monitoring and control.

4 Staff the new principal organization with competent, right-thinking and enthusiastic people with a high level of energy and the ability to carry development forward. Evaluate existing candidates and recruit from outside. Beware of inbreeding at the staffing stage! All too often you wind up with the same old chimps swinging on new vines.

5 Break the new managers to harness until they understand and can carry on your ideas, goals and strategies. You should run a series

of seminars so that everybody on the top two levels understands which way the organization as a whole is supposed to go.

6 Work out for each unit of the organization, be it production facility or staff function:
 – goals consistent with your overall goals;
 – strategies likewise linked to your own;
 – a table of organization;
 – staffing;
 – a programme of indoctrination.
 All this is analogous to points 1 to 3 above, which refer to the organization as a whole.

7 If necessary, continue the same procedure one step further down the organization to make sure that all employees understand their parts in the reoriented company. A process of change in the sequence described here will run more smoothly under strong central direction with adequate resources committed to the task. In this context, there are several important points to bear in mind:

(a) All decisions must be documented, accepted, agreed on and made known.

(b) Complete, open and accessible information must be given to as many people as possible. That includes employees, owners, customers and mass media. The information must be produced centrally, continuously and with the help of professional communicators. You are welcome to call it internal marketing if that helps.

(c) Produce a central training package as an aid to dissemination of new ideas, goals and strategies. Make sure that it is easy to understand, use concrete examples and make it fun.

(d) As a symbol of changes to come, you can make physical changes – redecorating, relocation, a new telephone directory or whatever.

(e) Do something about the jobs and people left over from the reshuffle. Re-educate them or release them. Set up goals in the form of commitments for each area of responsibility.

(f) Control instruments set up to monitor the organization usually lag behind in practice. It must be possible to measure the performance of individuals and units in ways that permit evaluation.

(g) Set up special training programmes for specific needs like profit control, customer service, quality control and languages.

(h) Equip a complete commando force to spearhead change, chase progress and troubleshoot as the programme moves forward. To be credible it must have access to, and include members of, the company's top management.

(i) It is absolutely essential that top management keeps a close check on developments and constantly makes sure that substantial and credible progress is being made. Top management must set a good example by observing the rules of the new organization.

(*j*) Opportunities for concrete change should be taken in the form of:
 - acquisitions and disinvestments
 - product renewal and development
 - celebration of important orders
 - public recognition and promotion of heroes
 - publicity for successes
 - rewards for achievement
 - publication of news; information is like love and money – people can never get enough

(*k*) Keep up the work of internal and external communication.

(*l*) Maintain a high top-management profile to encourage the workers.

(*m*) Rotate and fire executives as necessary.

The amount of energy available to bring about change in a company is usually much greater than expected. The importance of this fact cannot be over-emphasized, because a commitment to change involves a heavy investment in software, and that kind of investment decision is always much harder to make than a decision to invest in hardware like machines and buildings.

At one time it was believed that most individuals are automatically opposed to change. It has since been discovered that resistance to change varies according to the kind and degree of change and how it is accomplished. Strong resistance to change arises when:

 - the changes are drastic and radical
 - sudden and unexpected changes (shocks) occur
 - changes have adverse effect on those involved, who then regard themselves as losers
 - there is strong support for whatever it is (strategy, corporate mission, organization, etc) that is marked down for change
 - the reasons for making the change are unclear, causing unrest
 - previous changes have not turned out well

There is a theory based on organizational inertia. The concept of inertia is derived from physics, where it describes the tendency of an object to move in a straight line unless resisted or deflected by outside forces. The theory distinguishes between two kinds of organizational inertia:

1 Insight inertia.
2 Kinetic inertia.

Insight inertia refers to the forces that make it difficult for the organization or its leading persons to perceive problems. Kinetic inertia, on the other hand, refers to the hangups and blockages that hamper flexibility and create resistance to change.

The theory of dynamic conservatism holds that social systems struggle to remain what they are, to preserve the status quo. This is why organizations first ignore signals of change, then oppose change, try to counter its effects, and finally try to keep it confined within minimum bounds.

We can illustrate this by characterizing the development of social systems as proceeding from a stable state to one of unrest or turbulence, and from there to a new state of stability. The need for energy and driving force is great in the process of transition from stability to turbulence, but once the organization has been pushed over the hump, so to speak, the process continues under its own momentum.

An important fragment of knowledge related to processes of change is the ability of organizations to acquire new knowledge. All success in business depends ultimately on intensive and incessant learning. The organizations or individuals that are first to detect changes in the demand structures of customers and markets and to understand the motives that lie behind the changes are the ones that stand the best chance of succeeding.

Discussions of processes of change in organization have therefore increasingly come to focus on learning ability. Learning organizations are marked by early realization of problems, critical appraisal of their own mistakes, and a constant search for more effective behaviour patterns to maximize success. Such organizations review their corporate missions, try to find better techniques, methods and routines, and renew their visions, goals and strategies.

COMMUNICATION

Communication can be defined as the transmission of emotional or intellectual content.

Communication has acquired a high degree of importance in the new openness that has come to characterize business development and entrepreneurship. The technocratic managements of former epochs had a tendency to keep their corporate aims, missions and development plans as secret as possible. In contrast to this, we can now witness an openness that sometimes seems to go too far.

Communication has come to be important to business development in two ways. In the first place, leaders gather information by communicating with their environment and their own organization. Surprisingly often, ideas for effective business development are to be found within the organization itself. In the second place, communication is perhaps

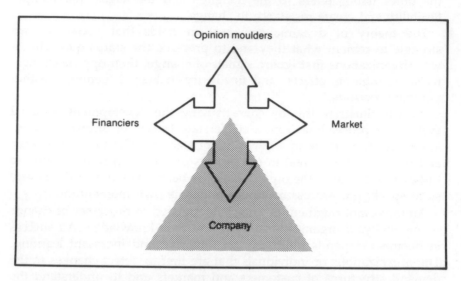

Figure 4 Communication model. The figure illustrates the principal target groups of corporate communications. In addition to marketing communication, companies nowadays must communicate with opinion moulders, with all their employees and with financiers, principally their owners. The most important kind of communication in business development is communication with one's own organization and the people in it; this applies to both the giving and receiving of information.

the most effective tool for achieving high efficiency in the strategies that are worked out.

The term communication implies a two-way flow where one party receives information and responds to it, either immediately or with a certain time-lag. Here is a communication model constructed by a communication consultancy firm:

Two factors are of fundamental importance in the outward communication of a strategic message from top management:

1 The quality of the message in terms of both content and form.
2 The quality of the medium used to convey the message (often the managing director of the company).

Communication of a strategic message requires different formulations for different target groups. Usually the chief executive is the main medium, and there is no effective substitute for a personal appearance by the top man. The form the message takes may vary considerably, from pithy slogans like 'The Businessman's Airline' or 'Management Data Consultants' to a lengthy and detailed document.

One way to explain a strategy is to translate it into operative terms.

If a corporate mission is expressed with a defined competitive edge and a rejuvenated product, the nature of the change is made clear. This also applies to changes in organization, investments in development, acquisitions and disinvestments, changes in cost and capital structures, changes in management philosophy and redefinition of markets and target groups.

You can also enhance the qualitative effect of communication by giving more or less detailed information to the same target group at different times. What you definitely must guard against is the risk of colouring the strategic message with rhetoric that is open to suspicion of insincerity. Cosmetic, populistic formulations like 'putting the customer first' are so hackneyed as to be meaningless. The gap between rhetoric and realism must be kept as narrow as possible.

One mistake that is sometimes made is over-communication at the wrong time. The employees of a company must, of course, receive some kind of regular information while a process of change is going on. The danger lies in telling them too much too soon, before you actually have anything of substance to say. Ambitious PR departments often fall into this trap, which benefits nobody. On the contrary, it may add to the unrest during the process of change, making it even harder to accomplish. A good tip, then, is to be careful of your timing; hold off until you have a meaningful message to deliver instead of trying to talk too soon about things that are unclear or irrelevant.

The media available for modern communication are many; but none of them is as effective as a personal appearance by the individual who embodies the process of change. That is why the ability to communicate is one of the most essential skills of leadership. Examples of media for strategic messages are:

- lectures
- seminars
- circulars
- documentation
- training programmes
- union branch discussions
- videotapes
- parties
- newspaper articles
- leadership development

The list could certainly be made longer. Target-group oriented training programmes are extremely effective, and leadership development programmes in conjunction with a process of change can be valuable in several ways. Everybody is exposed to the message and given an opportunity to study it in detail, and the idea of development can be linked to individual areas of responsibility.

Sometimes, unfortunately, communication becomes an end in itself. By this I mean that the message to be communicated has not been properly thought out, and the quantity of communication is used to disguise its poor quality.

In some situations form is more important than substance; this is truer in the United States, for example, than it is in Scandinavia. Formulation of the message must never be the main issue: the important thing is the intellectual substance of the message. Otherwise there is a strong risk that it will come out as empty blather that no-one will listen or pay attention to.

There is an old story of the vicar preparing his sermon for Sunday. Citing one particularly obscure passage in the Bible, he made a note in the margin: 'Weak argument. Raise voice.' Many communication situations are rather like that.

COMPANIZATION

The term companization is shorthand for breaking a function out of an organization and incorporating it as a separate company.

A wave of companization has rolled over Europe in the 1980s and 1990s. Three main motives can be distinguished:

1 Deregulation and privatization of public sector institutions have led to their being reorganized as limited companies.
2 A desire to increase the value of portfolios has also boosted companization.
3 Many heads of departments want to be their own bosses and lead their own companies.

It is of course very difficult to sell a business or part of a business unless it is operated as a company. Governments have therefore often found this type of legal entity very useful for purposes of deregulation.

There are many examples of stock-market-quoted companies that have been undervalued because the market has not been aware of the true value of their assets in real property, divisions or other operating units. It is of great instructive value to the market, and cash value to the owners, to isolate parts of the organization as companies. Another phenomenon is found in boom times: the desire of managers to create their own fiefs with all the attendant perquisites of title, pay and status. This was frequently a motive force for companization during the expansive 1980s especially in the data consultancy industry, for example.

Companization as such is a solution to an underlying problem, but sometimes it is treated as a solution to an as yet unidentified problem. It is therefore essential to be clear about the structure of motives behind a proposal to set up a company. Some of the motives that I have found relevant are listed below:

1 A functional unit has a large proportion (over 50 per cent) of external deliveries.
2 Preparation for sale of part of the business to other owners.
3 A function that was once strategically important to the business has become trivial and inefficient.
4 The core business is subject to restrictions that can be evaded by setting up a separate company.
5 The legal structure in a given environment requires the existence of a company with a board of directors, etc.
6 A tactical move in bargaining with unions.
7 Somebody needs or wants to put 'Managing Director' on his business card.
8 A desire for a higher degree of independence from principals.

It is thus advisable to define the motives for companization to avoid making it a solution in search of a problem.

COMPETITION

Competition is defined as 'rivalry or contest, often between two more or less well-matched contenders'. From the term competition we can derive many different concepts and models, all of them based on ability to compete, that is to be perceived as a better alternative than that offered by competing companies. Some of these concepts are described below.

Comparative advantage is a theory which holds that production of goods is subject to relative advantages or disadvantages that vary from one country to another, and that countries therefore benefit from specializing in the production of some goods, while importing others. This implies, for example, that even if a country is more efficient in absolute terms in producing two kinds of goods, it should opt to produce one and import the other.

An analogous situation is that of a trained business strategist who also happens to be the world's fastest typist. Just as the strategist can earn more money by developing business and paying someone else to do his typing, so can a country benefit from concentrating its resources on areas where its comparative advantage is greatest.

Competitive profile is a graph that compares the cost structures of a business unit with those of another. It highlights the areas in which the unit enjoys advantages of scale of one kind or another.

Competitive edge is what all (competitive) business strategies aim for. Many factors can give a competitive edge; they include more efficient production, ownership of patents, good advertising, good management and good customer relations. Long-term survival and expansion depend, in fact, on intensive and incessant learning. Willingness to absorb new knowledge provides the input needed for constant renewal of competitive edge.

Forces of competition are the factors that determine the state of competition in an industry. There are five of them:

1 Competition between existing companies.
2 The power of the buyer.
3 The power of the supplier.
4 The threat from new competitors.
5 Substitute products or services.

Competitive position is the position which a company occupies in its industry with reference to its present results and its strengths and weaknesses relative to its competitors. A business unit with a strong competitive position usually has a competitive edge protected by high entry barriers. Business units like that generally have a return on investment above the average for their industry.

Market share or relative market share (a company's share compared to its two or three strongest competitors) is often an essential component of competitive position.

Competitive strategy is a synonym for business strategy. It refers to the sum of the ways in which a business unit should behave in order to be competitive in its industry.

The term competition is used in many other contexts and combinations. Some examples are scope of competition, competitor analysis and competitor graphs. A constantly high learning capacity and creativity is an organization's best guarantee of sustained ability to compete.

COMPETITIVE EDGE

The whole object of business strategy is to gain a strategic advantage (or competitive edge). This strategic advantage should be of a kind that can be utilized as soon as possible and will last as long as possible.

Its function is to generate profits above the industry average and to gain market share.

Many industries, especially hi-tech hardware industries, have grown accustomed to finding a distinct competitive edge in the product itself. They can make rock drills that pound harder and faster, or ball bearings with small overall dimensions and finer tolerances than their competitors can make. If you can maintain a competitive edge through the intrinsic merits of your product, you are in a happy position. The main things you need in that situation are capable people in your research and development department, production and administrative departments. And your marketing must of course make your market aware of the competitive edge that lies in the product.

On the other hand you will not be required to demonstrate businessmanship in the sense of having to use your imagination to find a competitive edge in something other than the product. But that is exactly what more and more companies are having to do nowadays: to seek and find a competitive edge in something other than the product. There is a strong and growing demand for businessmanship in Sweden because more and more companies are being forced into competing on terms that lie outside the merits of the product itself. A few suggested approaches to the problem of finding or reinforcing a competitive edge might be:

1 Is your corporate mission outdated because customers' needs have changed?
2 Can you change the package of services that go with the hardware to make the total product more attractive?
3 How can you achieve profitability above the industry average?
4 Can you alter the division of labour in the industry by farming out or taking over some step in production?
5 What are the key issues that you need to identify and illuminate in order to improve your competitive position?
6 Can you find a competitive edge in a supporting function like information processing or distribution?

It is unfortunately all too easy to claim a competitive edge without taking the trouble to check whether the alleged advantage actually corresponds to what customers need. This leads you into 'Pepsodent with Irium' or 'Shell with ACI' or some other imaginary product benefit. It is essential to base your formulation of competitive edge on customers' needs, and to make sure that the supposed advantage really is an advantage from the customer's point of view.

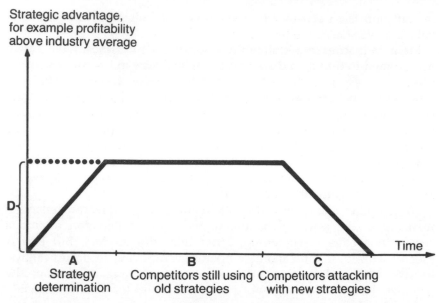

Strategic advantage,
for example profitability
above industry average

D

Time

A
Strategy
determination

B
Competitors still using
old strategies

C
Competitors attacking
with new strategies

Figure 5 Graph to illustrate the meaning of the term strategic advantage (competitive edge). **A** is the period during which the strategic advantage is developed, and **B** is the period during which competitors continue to stick to their old strategies. The length of **B** depends on the dynamics and nature of the industry concerned; there is naturally a great difference in reaction time between, say, service industries and heavy engineering industries. Period **C** is when competitors start to erode the competitive edge, while **D** on the vertical axis is the magnitude of the advantage, which can for example be expressed as percentage points of return on investment above the industry average.

In defining your own competitive edges, it is important to proceed from customers' need structures and to verify that the supposed advantage is actually perceived as a benefit by your customers.

CONTROL SYSTEMS

The heading to this entry really ought to be profit control systems, because the plain term 'control system' refers to the process of obtaining organized information about the extent to which operations are achieving their set goals. Surprisingly often, one finds that control systems are not congruent with the goal image. In many cases this is because the goal image has not been precisely defined in terms of money, or of quantities like orders received or market share, or of customer-perceived quality. If you have established the principal factors of quality as the customer perceives it, you can also measure and report on those factors without having to go out and ask customers so often that it causes undue expense to you or undue annoyance to them.

One of the commonest pitfalls is over-ambition in the construction of control systems. This may be because the designers of the system have set their sights too high, or because the criteria have been sloppily defined with the result that the designers try to satisfy too many demands without establishing what the users of the system actually need.

Such system failures often lead to prolonged and serious trouble that is very difficult to cure. One big company, three years after launching its control system, still had no follow-up reports in its organization, or at any rate none that the recipients bothered to read. Reporting discipline had declined to an abysmal level because the organization did not perceive reporting as meaningful as long as nothing came out of it. In that particular case the failure was due to over-ambition; they had tried to construct a system capable of solving all the information problems in a huge organization.

CORPORATE MISSION

A corporate mission (sometimes called business mission or business concept) is the opportunity for doing business that a company identifies in the context of needs, customers, products and competitive edge. The corporate mission concept has gained wide currency as an important part of an organization's ideological base. It is often used to arrive at a basic understanding and a holistic view of business relationships. At the same time, unfortunately, the many users of the term have diluted its meaning to the point where it has come to be regarded as a buzz-word.

In the context of corporate renewal, experience has shown that discussions of the parameters of corporate mission have been extremely fruitful and significant, regardless of whether the discussions have been part of something labelled a strategy development process or something else.

An important distinction that needs to be made early in any discussion of corporate mission is the distinction between a portfolio and a business unit. It is unnecessary to get entangled in confused attempts to define a corporate mission for groups of companies that have no real corporate mission. By this I mean that the various business units in a group may be satisfying different needs, possibly serving different companies with different products having different competitive advantages. I do not mean that a group should attempt to deny its organic origins: such a group may for example have grown up on a basis of expertise in chemicals, but does not necessarily have one corporate mission that fits all its members. On the other hand it may have a portfolio mission to utilize some shared resource to its common profit.

The following three points are an attempt to summarize the part that corporate mission plays in a corporate development process:

1 The process that leads to the formulation of a corporate mission is probably at least as important as the formulation itself, because it forces the management of a business unit to review the fundamental premises on which its operations are based.
2 The corporate mission clarifies the broad business picture that gives both management and employees in the organization the bird's-eye view essential to creation of long-term competitiveness.
3 A corporate mission has great communicative value, both internally in making the aims of the business clear to its employees, and externally for the information of shareholders, suppliers and customers.

The content of a corporate mission is defined below from three standpoints:

1 The mission must be relatively easy to define and relatively easy to communicate. A complicated corporate mission with many components is too difficult to explain to individuals inside and outside the organization.
2 The corporate mission must be based on benefit to the customer and the needs that the business satisfies in the market-place. In the 1950s and 1960s, corporate missions were often expressed in terms like 'Products & Services Ltd will manufacture and sell products and services to this group of customers and that.' Such a formula gives very little guidance to businesslike thinking.
3 It should be easy to answer the question 'Why should customers buy goods and services from us rather than from somebody else?'

The term corporate mission can be defined in terms of:

– needs
– customers
– product
– competitive edge

In determining a corporate mission you should start with the needs that your product satisfies on the market, or how what you do benefits your customers. In this context, the terms need, customer benefit and customer-perceived value can be considered as synonymous.

Determination of needs on the market you serve, that is the market you plan to sell to, requires much thought. You should try to discern the human needs behind the rational needs. The need for fast delivery of air freight for instance, is really an expression of the customer's

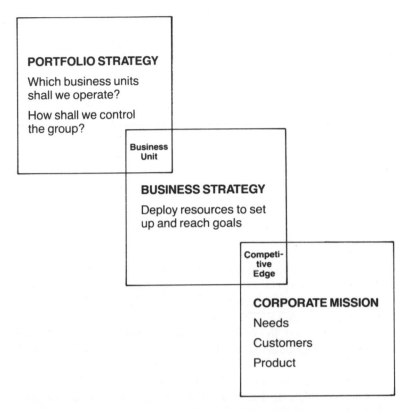

Figure 6 Corporate mission of SAS Cargo. 'SAS Cargo will provide fast and reliable transportation of goods to and from Scandinavia, thereby supporting the efforts of industry to reduce tied-up capital, and will provide transportation of emergency shipments.'

need to improve his profitability by reducing the amount of capital tied up in goods in transit.

By way of example, figure 6 shows the corporate mission formulated in 1983 for SAS Cargo.

There is a danger that a corporate mission may be formulated in general, non-committal terms and thus fail to guide the company in the intended direction. The corporate mission is part of a company's ideological base, an expression of the company's *raison d'être*. There is sometimes a tendency to equate corporate mission with strategy and vision. Even though the dividing lines are not hard and fast, it is often advisable to make a clear distinction.

One way to test the realism of your corporate mission is to ask a few check questions:

1 Is the company's business mission formulated with reference to customers' needs and demand, or to the need to keep its own production apparatus occupied?
2 Is the organization primarily concerned with customers' utility functions, or with its own and its employees' well-being?
3 Does its vision possess enough power, precision and stringency to involve and motivate the people in the organization?
4 Is development measurable in terms of the elements that define the corporate mission, or does it require an effort to achieve measurability and verification of progress?
5 Are the corporate mission, vision and strategies so well known and communicated that they guide the actions of the organization, both operative and strategic?

CREATIVITY

Psychological research into creativity has carefully avoided dealing with entrepreneurial ability as part of the concept of creativity. On the contrary, the predominant view for the past fifteen years has been that creativity and entrepreneurship must be carefully distinguished as two separate phenomena. This thesis, which still dominates thinking, has been questioned by many creativity researchers, who claim that psychologists have failed to understand the role of the entrepreneur in economic life.

By business creativity we generally mean the sum of a number of economic roles. On the one hand we have the worker who performs the operations, and on the other the capitalist who finances them. Between these two we can interpose the executive who administers ongoing operations.

In the view of many others, this is a static picture which focuses on routine operations and contains no creative elements at all. So it is perhaps not so surprising that the main body of creativity research has concentrated on scientific discoveries, technological inventions and works of art. If the business man is mentioned in the literature at all, he is seen as the person who uses the creative end-product in such a way as to make money and generate profit.

One of the commonest pitfalls is failure to distinguish between the capitalist and the entrepreneur. Although the two roles can be combined in the same person, analytically they stand for two totally different quantities. One reason for the confusion may be that the entrepreneur often makes money and thus takes on the aspect of a capitalist in the sense that he has made enough profit to finance his own operations.

To understand the analytical distinction we must define the role of the entrepreneur. Economic activity is the result of interaction between resources of several kinds, which are collectively known as production factors. The classic production factors are property, labour and capital. But to produce anything, these resources must be combined by somebody who makes allocating decisions. These decisions involve determining what is to be produced, how it is to be produced, what resources are required, and what needs the product is to satisfy.

These decisions are made by an entrepreneur. He is thus the person who ultimately decides how and for what purpose certain resources shall be used. However, the action resulting from the decision on use of resources presupposes some kind of business innovation, that is the discovery of an opportunity to do business or in other words to make profitable use of resources. For this reason, entrepreneurship consists in the discovery of how profitable operations can be carried on, combined with the ability to allocate resources to take advantage of the business opportunity.

Entrepreneurship is thus not a matter of running a business, nor of owning capital or companies. The entrepreneurial element is the ability to discover and take advantage of opportunities for business. Defined in this way entrepreneurship has many traits in common with creativity.

The definition of the term creativity is vague and tends to vary, but most researchers are agreed that it comprises an end-product and a cognitive process leading to the end-product. The term creativity has been used so loosely by so many that it needs to be defined: 'Creativity is the ability to integrate discrete elements of knowledge in new, innovative ways to create hitherto unknown combinations.'

Business opportunities arise in two ways:

1 Discovery of a way of satisfying customers' needs which is better than the currently available alternatives.
2 Imperfections in the market that lead to pure arbitrage operations, that is trader or merchant buys in one market at one price while simultaneously selling to another market at another price.

Traditional models of competition place the emphasis on the competitive aspect. My hypothesis is that the competitive aspect is of secondary importance to the entrepreneur, while the creative aspect – the finding of a way that leads to better satisfaction of customers' needs – is the real force that drives him. Having made this business innovation, he turns his attention to competing with the alternatives currently on the market.

To further distinguish the entrepreneurial role from other phenomena, we can consider the following example. A person possessing special knowledge of market conditions in a particular industry may be employed in a company where his knowledge is put to profitable use. If that individual works for a salary rather than uses his knowledge on his own account, the entrepreneur is the employer, not the knowledgeable employee. The employer was the one who was enterprising enough to hire a person possessing the knowledge in question.

Entrepreneurial discovery always requires a period of divergence. This is needed to sort out the elements of knowledge that characterize a given situation. During this period the creative person frees himself from the existing framework that inhibits innovation. The creative person must establish a new pattern of ends and means and acquire a total picture of the components of which his creation will consist. This is followed by a phase of convergent thinking, of assembling the creation and setting up the administrative process that leads to a business operation.

Creative processes require periods of intense concentration on all components of the problem. These periods must be interrupted by longer periods during which the problem receives more diffuse attention, to be succeeded by another brief period of intense concentration, and so on. This is one of the reasons why business development process can hardly ever be concentrated in time or compressed with regard to resources. Development projects of a business nature require a certain amount of calendar time. As a business development consultant, I often have to explain this to clients who sometimes think that six months of sporadic activity can be replaced by one month of concentrated work. That is just not possible if you want to utilize creative resources in a process of development.

CULTURE

The term corporate culture has gained wider currency as a result of the rethinking that has taken place in recent years. The term is often used loosely, so it will be as well to define it here. The concept is described here from two standpoints: the first refers to the values that prevail within an organization, and the second refers to the cultural patterns surveyed by the Dutch researcher Geerte Hofstede, with special reference to differences between national cultures. The latter has proved to be highly relevant in view of the current internationalization and globalization of business.

The received interpretation of the concept of culture addresses the inward life of an organization: the way it lives, thinks, acts and is. It may be a matter of how decisions are made, or how employees are rewarded and penalized. It considers communication within the organization, and tolerance of opposition. It may even include more peripheral phenomena such as organization of leisure activities, attitudes to

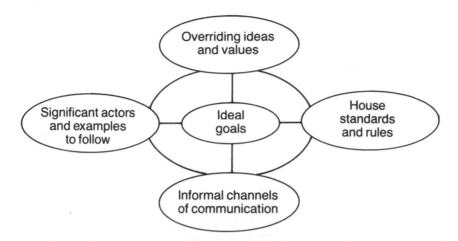

Figure 7 Corporate culture. A corporate culture can be illustrated like this. The idea for the figure is derived from *Integrerad organisationslära* (*Integrated Organization Theory*) by Lars H. Bruzelius and Per-Hugo Skärvad.

the opposite sex or attitudes to the accumulation of status symbols like cars, car telephones and personal computers.

Interest in the culture of organizations has increased sharply in recent years, partly because of a growing realization of how much cultural phenomena influence the success and efficiency of an organization. Many researches report that successful companies have strong corporate cultures, which are the result of a deliberate effort to develop an *esprit de corps* for the benefit of all concerned. Some examples of actors that influence corporate culture are:

– ideal goals
– prevailing ideas and values
– significant personalities and role models
– standards and rules
– informal channels of communication

A more business-oriented specification would read:

– importance of work to success in business
– risk-taking, rewards and penalties
– energy, drive and initiative
– intelligence and training
– respect for human beings as a resource in general, and for employees in particular as contributors to success in business
– recognition that customers and their needs are the point upon which business turns

What is usually meant by corporate culture, however, is the attitudes, opinions and behaviour patterns through which these basic values are expressed. Corporate culture can be considered as a manifestation of the values that are expressed in, and influence such things as, organizational structure and personnel recruitment.

The hallmark of 'excellent companies' (a term coined by Peters and Waterman, 1982) is a symbiosis between business strategy and corporate culture. Deep involvement and devotion to work are often inward criteria for success in business.

The second sense of the term corporate culture can best be described by summarizing the findings of Geert Hofstede concerning cultural differences between countries published in *Culture's Consequences* (1980).

Hofstede's model has the advantage of having high explanatory value and of being easy to apply. He classifies the cultural patterns of organizations according to four variables:

1 *Individualism/Collectivity* Individualistic cultures assume that the individual acts in his own interest or in the interest of those closest to him, that is his family. Collective cultures, on the other hand, assume that a person belongs by birth or employment to a more or less cohesive group from which the individual cannot free himself. The group looks after the interests of the individual, requiring total and unquestioning obedience in return. This can be considered a kind of sectarianism in which the interests of the group dictate the behaviour of its members.

2 *Power distance* The remoteness of power as a cultural characteristic defines the extent to which less powerful individuals in a group accept inequality of power and regard it as a normal state of affairs. Inequality exists in all cultures, but there is great variation in willingness to accept the remoteness of power. If we consider nations, we can take variation in incomes as a yardstick of the prevailing remoteness of power. In companies, the criteria include not only pay and ownership of an interest, but also status symbols like the standard of company cars, private chauffeurs, and how easy or difficult it is to talk to the boss.

3 *Avoidance of uncertainty* This variable indicates the extent to which people strive to avoid situations in which they feel insecure, for example by enforcing strict standards of behaviour and subscribing to a belief in absolute truths. One can turn the reasoning around and ask to what extent individuals in the culture are perturbed by situations which seem to be unstructured, unclear or unpredictable.

Cultures that dislike insecurity are active, aggressive, emotional and intolerant, whereas cultures that accept insecurity are more reflective, less aggressive, stolid and relatively tolerant.

4 *Masculinity/Femininity* This variable indicates the extent to which a culture accepts traits that are thought to be characteristic of feminine behaviour. Virtually all cultures are male-dominated, and in masculine cultures males are expected to be self-assured, ambitious, competitive and oriented towards material success. Men respect and are drawn towards that which is big, strong and swift. In masculine cultures, females are expected to take care of matters connected with the quality of life, as well as of infants and the aged and infirm.

Femininity thus implies in Hofstede's terminology a willingness to accept that which is small, weak and slow.

To put it briefly, masculine cultures are characterized by the pursuit of material success and decisiveness. Feminine cultures, on the other hand, are characterized by the pursuit of life quality and care for the weak.

Scandinavia is an extreme example in so far as Scandinavians in general exhibit a high degree of individuality, are not remote from their leaders, cope well with insecurity and have a strongly feminine culture as defined by Hofstede. In this they are quite unlike Germans or Americans. Even though they too are individualists, their leaders are more remote from the people, they have a greater need for firm structures and are less willing to accept insecurity, and they are more masculine.

These differences are not always recognized. That is why Swedish management culture often fails in the United States, and why the Finnish style of management raises hackles in Sweden. The same differences are strongly relevant to the way a process of business development is managed in a company and how entrepreneurship works. You cannot operate an extremely decentralized business development process in a culture that is accustomed to doing things by the book. In many cases a tendency to ask rather than order is interpreted as a sign of weakness, which undermines leadership.

Conversely, the role of the one wolf – the strong, individualistic entrepreneur – is open to question. Group-oriented entrepreneurship may be much more effective than the one-man-band variety. In places like Japan and Scandinavia, where group dynamics are held in high esteem, the process of development may get better long-term results than in the United States, where the lone, strong, resourceful hero is the corporate development ideal.

Hofstede's model is highly relevant to an assessment of work organizations, and to comparisons between both organizations and nations.

CUSTOMERS

By customers, we mean regular buyers of goods or services. Potential customers are usually included in the abstract concept of the market. All business depends on customers, on buyers who come back to buy again.

The customer was not nearly so important during the years from the end of World War II to the mid-1970s as he is today. When demand exceeded supply, much less attention was paid to the customer's wishes than has been the case since the mid-1970s. Customers were formerly regarded as an abstract mass who were charged handling fees and subjected to a rationalization process designed to make them buy as much as possible every time they placed an order. Producers put their own production apparatus first and tried to adapt customer behaviour to it.

Since the mid-1970s, producers have had to focus their attention on the customer and his need structures in order to influence customer demand for their products. Large corporations still have a tendency to treat the customer as an abstraction. Comet-like careers in big organizations tend to make high-ranking executives neglect finding out who their customers actually are and to get acquainted with them and their underlying need structures. In this case, the term customer refers to executives and individuals who make or influence buying decisions.

It is sometimes difficult to identify the customer in the sense of identifying the need structures to be satisfied, especially where you have dealer structures, which are becoming increasingly common. In the transport business you have to ask yourself whether it is the needs of the shipper or those of the freight agent that you must satisfy. In the travel business the same question arises with respect to travellers and travel agents. Industries that have been accustomed to dealing directly with end users and original equipment manufacturers (OEMs), because of the specialized technical nature of their products, are now facing a different situation. As products take on the nature of commodities, dealers (agents and distributors are the same thing) begin to come into the picture for both mining equipment and ball bearings. It then becomes necessary to learn the need structures of the new customers, that is of the dealers.

Over the last ten years there has been much talk of 'putting the customer in the centre', 'our customers are our greatest asset', and so on. Though such phrases can correctly be applied to all kinds of business, they are all too apt to become just phrases unless they are given a concrete meaning. A bank or an airline that claims to take good care of its customers must mean that it does so at least as well as its competitors, otherwise the claim is just so much hot air.

The new recognition of the importance of the customer is a good thing, but we must beware of letting it stop at lip service only.

DECENTRALIZATION

A process of decentralization is under way almost everywhere, in both business and public administration. The aim of this process is to make operations more efficient by having decisions made close to the customer by people who know the market well.

There are two main motives for the wave of decentralization:

1 Decentralization makes a company more market-oriented and thus more efficient.
2 It encourages motivation, entrepreneurship and job satisfaction.

Decentralization is highly desirable in times of prosperity. It is easy to accept delegated responsibility when success is assured. But decentralization is not such an unmixed blessing in times of adversity. Responsibility is not so easy to assume when it becomes necessary to make hard decisions, maybe to fire colleagues, and to take a tight grip on costs.

The main driving force for decentralization, in my opinion, is growing pressure of competition. When such pressure is low in a seller's market, there is much less need for market orientation. The brainwork in companies can be concentrated to top management, and the organization is expected to act on command after somebody else has done the thinking. When pressure of competition hardens, this is an extremely inefficient way to lead a company. Substantive decision-making is too far removed from customers, who then turn to more agile organizations that can make quick decisions. Decentralization of decision-making then becomes a matter of self-preservation and ability to compete.

A further reason for the desirability of decentralization has been that the number of thinking people in a well-educated middle class has increased in most countries. People are no longer conditioned to obedience, but question every decision that is made. For that reason it has been found much more efficient to distribute corporate brainwork and get more people to think and make decisions, primarily in the interests of customer-perceived quality.

My conclusion is that decentralization is an admirable means of increasing efficiency in the utility dimension, but that it does not work nearly so well in the cost dimension. This is evident from the public sector and those parts of private business which have now been forced to get their costs down.

There is an analytical approach to the issue of decentralization and centralization which was originally proposed by C. K. Pralahad and Yves L. Doz in a book on global organization entitled *The Multinational Mission*. I myself have used the Pralahad-Doz analysis, supplemented by a couple of points, on several occasions. This analytical method can be briefly described as comprising four questions:

1 Which essential functions ought to be kept together from the standpoint of overall strategy?
2 Which functions call for local adaptability and closeness to the customer?
3 Where do the advantages of large-scale operation lie, and what is the position with regard to economies of scale and the Experience Curve?
4 How is the motivation of leaders and other people affected?

In non-competitive systems, of which there are many, a kind of anarchistic decentralization can be made to work. By this I mean that an organization is fragmented into small pieces with no analysis of efficiency.

A Pralahad-Doz analysis reveals bad structures in an organization, especially one that is in transition from a non-competitive to a competitive environment. The question of division of responsibilities in an organization is likewise illuminated by this type of analysis. One difficulty in implementing the analysis is that of striking a balance between large-scale operation, where economically justified, on the one hand and decentralization and motivation on the other. The lines for economy-of-scale advantages and motivating factors intersect somewhere. In my opinion much progress has been made if analyses of this kind are so competently carried out that people understand the pros and cons. Let me illustrate this with a recent example.

An organization that had been largely shielded from competition was gradually, over a period of years, moving to a condition of unrestricted competition. Local initiatives had been taken in many parts of its decentralized structure in the area of product development as well as in marketing, service level, etc. It was possible to make a fairly good estimate of the extra costs incurred by this anarchistic decentralized system, and it was thus also possible to explain to members of the organization what their current behaviour was costing it.

An in-depth analysis revealed that the primary tasks of the decentralized structure were sales and after-sales service. There was no difficulty about persuading the organization of the need for certain issues such as product development, strategy and marketing to be dealt with centrally.

The great hazards of organization rationality are

1 co-ordination mania;
2 compromise;
3 inflated cost levels;
4 lack of flexibility.

The dilemma of organization that always calls for 'manual control' is the dichotomy between rational, large-scale, co-ordinated solutions on the one hand and the efficiency-boosting effects of small-scale entrepreneurship on the other. It is a sound general rule that decentralized entrepreneurship is a good thing in good times, whereas many questions require a strong central hand in bad times.

DEREGULATION

Deregulation, in a strategic context, refers to industries or areas where competition was formerly strictly limited by legislation and where the limitations are eased or abolished. The classic case with which most people associate the word is the deregulation of air passenger traffic in the United States, initiated in 1978 by the Carter administration. Deregulation of telecommunications in the United States and of banking and currency trading in Western Europe have since come to highlight a new kind of strategic situation that scarcely existed before 1978.

To understand deregulation and the business opportunities it offers, one should first try to understand the factors that led to the regulations being imposed in the first place, and how things have changed since that happened. In the case of airline traffic, it was considerations of safety that made governments all over the world feel, after World War II, that regulation was necessary. The underlying idea was that unrestricted competition would tempt airlines to cut corners on safety.

What has happened since then is that safety in aviation has steadily improved and has now reached a level that would once have been almost inconceivable. Since the beginning of the 1960s, with the exception of 1985, the number of scheduled airline passengers killed in accidents has fallen steadily per passenger-kilometre or by any other yardstick you care to name.

Many of the regulated monopolies were originally set up because the technologies and investments involved made competition impossible. Telecommunications were long regarded as a 'natural' monopoly, but modern radio technology, optic fibre cables strung along railway lines, etc. have made the business an attractive investment proposition for new operators. This creates problems for the former monopolists, one of which is how to generate a sense of success in their organizations. Being forced to yield market shares causes psychological and organizational upsets of an often unforeseen kind.

I repeat: deregulation needs to be analysed with reference to the factors that originally led to regulation.

The disadvantages of regulation had grown more and more apparent in the light of the huge improvement in efficiency that has taken place in private enterprise throughout the world, partly as a result of the energy crisis of the mid–1970s. It has become increasingly obvious that productivity is decidedly poorer in regulated industries. This is of course due to the deadwood that organizations accumulate when they do not have to worry about competition. As national economies have got deeper into trouble, the inefficiency of regulated industries has become more and more of an embarrassment. This is probably one of the main explanations of the wave of deregulation now sweeping the Western world.

Perhaps the most significant observation to be made here is that ability and will to compete is atrophied in deregulated industries compared to other industries. This lack of competitiveness naturally occurs not only in production, i.e. in cost per unit produced, but just as much on the other axis of efficiency, i.e. value as a function of utility and price. The 'soft' customer utility functions on the service side are often underdeveloped. This is natural and understandable in an environment shielded from competition.

Spectacular improvements in productivity can be observed in the deregulated industries, clear evidence that regulation causes inefficiency due to lack of competition.

According to all the theories, a company in a monopoly position ought to generate abnormally high profits. But such is hardly ever the case in practice, because companies that are shielded from competition let their cost levels drift upward through a surfeit of capital and costs to the point where their profits are not much better. This is generally reflected in low value-added per employee, and a low level and low standards of performance.

Deregulation research is a relatively new discipline which has arisen mainly in the United States and the United Kingdom.

DEVELOPMENT

Development can be described as change from a more primitive to a more sophisticated state. In a glossary of terms associated with business, development definitely rates a place today. The term is used in two senses:

1 To denote one of the four basic functions of a company (the other three being marketing, production and administration).

2 To denote a method of tackling issues that gets things moving in the right direction.

The development function (or department) in a company usually devotes its effort to product development, or to concept development in the case of software industries. This is what we naturally associate with the word development.

In recent times a couple of other terms have come into use which compete with the traditional use of the word development in industry. One is market development, which refers to expansion of existing clientele, and the other is organization development, which refers to the development of individuals, groups, areas of responsibility, control systems, incentives and so on.

Nevertheless, by far the most common meaning of the word development is still the development of goods and services in the company to satisfy customers' underlying need structures and thereby increase demand for one's own product.

The second sense of the term development can be most simply explained by contrasting it to dealing with problems of administration. Matters that are dealt with are matters that call attention to themselves. They arise in every kind of activity. Prices must be adjusted, employees must be recruited, budgets must be drawn up, reports must be read. Dealing with issues is the main function of administrative management, or what Joseph Schumpeter calls static efficiency.

The characteristic feature of development issues, on the other hand, is that you have to go out and look for them. They do not arise spontaneously, but require an input of energy to get results. Development issues have acquired a marked degree of prominence with the transition from shop-minding management to more dynamic management. It is often an effective approach to try to identify the right development issues to follow up in your own business. By highlighting them, you can get a better appreciation of what needs to be changed and developed in order to improve the quality of the business.

In a modern business development process, you cannot take it for granted that development resources should be used to improve product performance. In many cases they should be devoted to other functions instead, the ones where the company can most easily identify competitive edges that give increased satisfaction of customer need structures and thereby improve the company's ability to compete. Business development is, in short, a matter of allocating resources to where they will produce the greatest possible competitive edge for the longest possible time.

The ability to handle development issues is what characterizes modern management. Maximum efficiency in administering the status quo has given way to efficiency in developing one's area of responsibility. The business development concept has come to be a characteristic of offensive strategies designed to make the business grow rather than to conserve its resources. Both ingredients are of course necessary to successful business management. The newly discovered development aspect of business management sometimes tempts managers into flamboyancy and rash use of resources, which is not a good thing.

DISTRIBUTION

The dictionary gives two definitions for distribution:

1 Agreed or regular allocation and delivery of goods.
2 The totality of operations undertaken to make goods or services available to customers.

The term distribution had wide currency at the end of the 1950s and during the 1960s, when shortages of goods in most western countries gave way to surpluses. The production component of the price of goods fell, and the concept of marketing arose. At that time, the term distribution was often used as a synonym for marketing, and terminological confusion prevailed.

In modern usage, the term distribution has tended to revert to its original meaning of physical movement of goods. In this sense, the term distribution comprises two aspects:

1 Service level in terms of availability of goods to customers.
2 Management of resources with respect to tied-up capital and transportation costs.

The essential thing is to make it clear which sense of the word you are using.

DIVERSIFICATION

The idea of diversification has a varied history. It was in high fashion in connection with corporate development in the late 1960s and early 1970s, but fell on hard times when concentration on principal business gained the upper hand over diversification. The reason is, of course, the globalization and other manifestations of economies of scale that have affected many industries.

In more recent times, diversification, now in a more sober guise, has once more become topical, but this time for different reasons. Many companies are now generating so much capital from their principal business, and finding a lack of opportunities for further expansion within that business, that diversification seems a useful way to invest their capital and spread their risks.

If we look back briefly at the history of diversification, we can identify the undue faith placed in plug-in technocratic management capability by practically all industries as the main reason for the popularity of diversification in the 1960s. One of the tenets of that faith was that intimate knowledge of the industry concerned was irrelevant to the exercise of management: generalized management skills could be applied equally well to any industry.

Now diversification is making a comeback, but not for the same reasons. More business-oriented managements have arisen with the ability and the courage to diversify, and there are businesses with strong, positive cash flows that are seeking opportunities for risk-spreading and profitable investment. Realization of the importance of trade logic to success in business can now help to avoid the mistakes that once caused diversification to fall into disrepute.

In the context of diversification it is advisable to ask yourself why you are doing it. The possible answers are:

– to spread risks, that is to equalize your financial position over a period of time
– for financial reasons, because you believe it will pay off better than other ways of investing your money
– because synergies with your present business will benefit the whole to an extent that justifies diversification.
– for entrepreneurial reasons, simply because you regard the risk inherent in diversification as an exciting challenge.

EFFICIENCY

The word efficiency is bedevilled by much the same linguistic vagueness as, for example, the word strategy. What it really means is value created in relation to productivity. Value is the relationship between utility and price, while productivity is the relationship between number of units produced and cost. Improving efficiency thus means creating more value with the same productivity, or the same value with better productivity, or a combination of both.

The term efficiency is often, but incorrectly, used as a synonym for cost reduction and productivity. Cost reduction is naturally an important component of efficiency, but it is not the same thing because it ignores the value factor. Productivity can be defined as number of units produced per unit of cost consumed. But productivity says nothing about creation of value. You may have a very productive

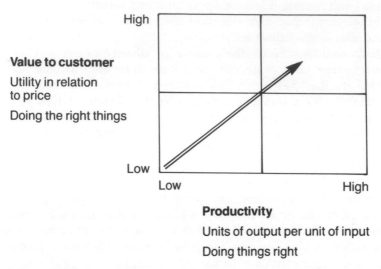

Value to customer

Utility in relation
to price

Doing the right things

Productivity

Units of output per unit of input

Doing things right

Figure 8 Efficiency matrix.

operation manufacturing steam engines, i.e. you may be turning them
out at low cost in terms of man-hours and capital, but your operation
is still not efficient because nobody wants to buy steam engines.

The Trabant car has come to be a symbol of the inability of planned
economies to achieve efficiency. However great the productivity
attained in the manufacture of Trabants, efficiency remains abysmally
low because the cars are unsaleable except as souvenirs or inverted
status symbols. (Trabants currently fetch high prices in the UK, where
a kind of cult has grown up around them.)

Sustained profitability is by far the best criterion of efficiency in a
company. The same applies to a business portfolio, but it is much
harder to measure efficiency in departments of companies, in public-
sector bodies and in other organizations. How, for example, can a
trade union measure its efficiency? The obvious answer, of course, is
that it should try to assess the amount of utility it creates for its
members in relation to the dues those members pay.

The basic parameters of efficiency are illustrated in Figure 8. Value
to the customer is the function of utility and price. Utility can be
broken down into a number of utility functions of which price, paradoxically, is an indicator. Productivity, as we see, is the function of
output of goods and services and the cost incurred in producing them.
A high value in relation to productivity is meaningless, as is high
productivity unrelated to creation of value.

Strategic issues are ones of broad and long-term significance. The
distinction between strategic and operative is one of degree rather

than of kind. The strategic perspective is determined partly by the need for long-term thinking in the industry concerned, and partly by the degree of financial or other foresightedness allowed the company or organization by its owners.

Inefficiency seems to have an inevitable logic of its own. Inefficiency always leads to slackness, bureaucracy, decadence. This seems to apply equally to ideologies, nations and trade unions. The consequence of sustained inefficiency is that the *raison d'être* of the organization is called in question, which eventually leads to either its disappearance or a takeover by another owner or principal with more ambition or competence.

In a protected environment such as a planned economy, these consequences are delayed. Many organizations can continue to exist without creating any apparent value in relation to what they cost. In the absence of a free market capable of making its own decisions, there is no signalling system to trigger the Darwinian process which Joseph Schumpeter called 'creative destruction'.

Strategy development and processes of renewal are harder to accomplish in the public sector than in organizations exposed to competition. In the latter, the inflow of revenues and profits is a highly reliable indicator of efficiency. Many other types of organization – not only government agencies and the like – lack this indicator. Without it, the organization has less incentive to find new paths, and any process of change that is initiated tends to remain merely an intellectual exercise. The new spirit of the age, the movement towards efficiency and personal performance orientation, together with the collapse of the planned economies, has caused leaders to look harder for reference points by which to gauge their efficiency.

Departments within companies have exactly the same kind of problem as public-sector bodies. The users of their services have no alternative source of supply, and they themselves have no alternative outlet. Such units naturally have great difficulty in assessing their own efficiency, and special methods, also applicable to public ˜administration, have therefore been developed.

An important point to bear in mind in this context is of course that many people now in positions of leadership are far from being performance-oriented: they may be more interested in consolidating their power of position, or they may be relation-oriented and view efficiency simply as a threat to good relations with people in their immediate surroundings.

As things are going in Europe, failure to do anything about efficiency is like committing three of the Seven Deadly Sins: Lechery, Gluttony and Sloth. They, too, feel good initially, but after a while they lose their charm. This is a fate that is now befalling many of those who have chosen the path of procrastination, who have been too lazy to do the things they know they ought to do.

ENTREPRENEURSHIP

The entrepreneurial person carries a high charge of energy and is motivated, action-oriented and sensitive to results. The entrepreneur can be identified by a number of characteristic traits. He or she:

- prefers to make their own decisions
- appreciates risk-taking
- wants to see the results of what s/he does and expects constructive criticism and praise
- wants to be able to take an active part in business, and is therefore often happiest in small organizations
- likes quick development and innovation
- flourishes in expansive conditions and a business-oriented environment
- makes great demands on themself and on the abilities of associates

In contrast to the environmental factors that stimulate entrepreneurship, here are some things that entrepreneurial people seldom suffer gladly:

- stagnation and lack of progress
- bureaucracy and complicated routines
- planning and consultation
- argument, tactics and diplomacy

This implies that the entrepreneur is not necessarily a good administrator or long-term planner, or a good chief executive of a large company where personnel management skills are needed. S/he is often not at all personnel-oriented, and is reluctant to delegate because s/he generally believes s/he can do things best themself. As a result, the entrepreneurial person is often a misfit in large corporate environments, and tends to avoid them.

The entrepreneur is a creative, imaginative and energetic person. S/he is often flamboyant and self-willed, and is therefore easily repelled by administrative corporate cultures.

The importance of the entrepreneurial person to the launching and growth of companies cannot be overemphasized. Everybody in our companies and organizations needs to be made aware of the qualities of that kind of person as soon as possible.

The attention and energy of the entrepreneur are always directed towards getting a result, reaching a goal, regardless of what it is s/he is doing. It may be building a boat, learning to play the piano, passing an examination, starting a company or reorganizing an administrative unit in a company. S/he has a force of volition that drives them.

We can see the same kind of thing in the world of sport. It is not outstanding physical prowess that decides the day, but usually the force of volition that drives a sportsman or sportswoman to train and practise until he or she can beat all comers.

To understand how knowledge of entrepreneurship can be utilized, we must go back to human motivation and study that concept in greater depth.

Sociological studies show that there has been a great growth of entrepreneurship in Europe in recent years. The number of people who consider themselves capable of starting a company has increased, and entrepreneurship has become a means of self-realization. These new potential entrepreneurs feel a strong need to succeed and want to prove their abilities by competing and winning. They regard the money they make in the process as a sign of success rather than as a means of exercising power.

The traditional entrepreneur was a loner who stubbornly and persistently pursued the realization of a business concept, whereas the new entrepreneurs are much stronger on relations and attach much greater importance to human relations and social contacts. They are not purely careerists or climbers, but are capable of interacting with their human environment.

FUNCTIONAL STRATEGY

Figure 9 illustrates what is meant by a management function (normally organized as a department of a company). Functional strategy is a term that is often used; it means the direction followed by a function or department in line with the overall strategy of the business unit to which it belongs. The term functional strategy has acquired great importance nowadays because it gives rise to strategic thinking at a level which was formerly subject to direct control, a control by rules and instructions within the framework of a defined corporate mission.

Extending the work of strategy down to the functional level gives a completely different feel for business in the company and offers a much greater choice for recruitment to executive positions that call for business knowledge. Functional strategy means doing the right things within the framework of a given function.

Functional strategy is therefore the orientation of a function (department) to align it with business strategy in a way that everybody concerned perceives as a logical way to do their work. Formulation of that kind of functional strategy is a neglected area in many companies. Functions like personnel and electronic data processing (EDP) have

Figure 9 Functional strategy. The basic business strategy is formulated on the basis of the corporate mission and is then broken down into functional strategies for the company's various departments or functions. Formulation of functional strategies along these lines is a neglected area of business management that could probably yield great gains in efficiency. With proper attention to functional strategy it is possible to influence with great precision both the value of a function's output and the resources needed to achieve that output.

traditionally had difficulty in tying in their operations with business strategies; this is much easier for functions like information, development and marketing.

We must also recognize that the importance of a given function can vary from time to time. The marketing function was very important in the 1960s. Finance, personnel and EDP became more important during the 1970s. And in the 1980s it was information that was regarded as the most important function.

When you undertake a review of strategy in, say, your marketing department or accounting department, it is advisable to run an audit of the department. By this I mean a study and critical evaluation of the resources consumed by the department in relation to what it produces. The audit should be completely unbiased. A few essential points you should bear in mind when working out a functional strategy are:

1 Define the role of the function and what it is required to do.
2 Make sure that the manager of the function understands your corporate mission.
3 Specify how the function contributes to your business.
4 Draw up clear lines of demarcation between functions.
5 If you can, review all functions at the same time.
6 Direct the energies of the function towards the corporate mission, so that they are not sidetracked into functional professionalism.
7 Balance professional competence, professional ethics and businessmanship in a way that does not give rise to conflicts.

An ideal functional unit should be both productive and efficient: it should do what it does well, and it should have a worked-out functional strategy linked to the business strategy of the business unit.

FUNCTIONS OF BUSINESS MANAGEMENT

There are four basic functions of business management, which reflect the phases of the business cycle. They are:

1 Development.
2 Marketing.
3 Production.
4 Administration.

This simple classification is often highly instructive, for these basic functions apply to all types of company and all types of business unit.

DEVELOPMENT comprises the development of products and markets as well as of the organization and the people in it. Development implies adaptation to needs and is essential in all business activities.

MARKETING (see MARKET) is the business of creating demand. Without demand, arising from the need structures of customers, business cannot exist. The term marketing also includes selling, that is securing orders.

PRODUCTION is the total process of making the goods and performing the services that customers demand and of bringing them to the customer. Distribution may belong to the production or marketing function depending on the type of industry and the importance of the distribution aspect to business.

ADMINISTRATION covers all the actions required to control resources. In a business unit, the term administration comprises all the supporting functions necessary to doing business.

GOALS AND VISIONS

Several different terms are used to describe the level of ambition set for an activity. Management by vision is a term that has come into wide currency recently; it means motivating people to work towards an ideal state of affairs.

Vision, in the sense of something seen in a dream, is the term used to describe a picture of a relatively remote future in which business has developed under the best of possible conditions and in accordance with the hopes and dreams of the owner or chief executive. A vision provides a benchmark for what one hopes to achieve in business, and can be a guide to the level of ambition of strategic planning.

Vision has come to play an increasingly important part in the process of change in modern business. The term is intimately associated with entrepreneurial behaviour and a high level of ambition, which is one of the reasons for its growth in importance. One purpose of a vision is to set up a yardstick for achievement of goals extending into the future, against which present performance can be compared. Yet perhaps the most important purpose of a vision is to give work a meaningful content and thereby create motivation and involvement among all the people in the company. A vision, moreover, is a much more diffuse component of a company's set of goals than the other, more quantifiable, goals. A vision need never in fact be realized, but can and should be revised as results are achieved. Hickman and Silva (1984) describe a vision as: 'Essentially, a vision is a mental journey from the known to the unknown, creating the future from a montage of current facts, hopes, dreams, dangers and opportunities.' A vision can be said to link business with corporate culture, creating a common standard of values for the individual performance of employees.

Level of ambition is the performance motivation that impels the head or management of a company in stating the results of strategic planning. One of the commonest causes of conflict within management is that the levels of ambition of, say, a department head and his superior are out of step. I have seen cases in which an energetic chief executive had evidently set performance goals on the basis of his own level of ambition without securing the concurrence of his immediate subordinates. Dissatisfaction from above and frustration from below are a common pattern of reactions.

Goal is used here as a portmanteau term to denote the concrete results of visions and levels of ambition, and the criteria against which the success of strategies will eventually be evaluated. Goals should perhaps in the first instance be expressed as levels of performance to be achieved in serving customers. Goals expressed in this way can motivate people in the organization; it is more difficult to do so with profitability criteria like return on equity. Goals should thus be expressed in different terms in such a way as to inspire enthusiasm.

The purpose of explaining visions, levels of ambition and goals is to raise the level of performance of the organization by involving people in more meaningful activity.

A goal picture should have at least four dimensions:

1 Economic goals.
2 Quantitative goals.
3 Qualitative goals.
4 Development goals.

The economic aspect is obviously necessary, but people are unlikely to work up enthusiasm for goals stated in terms of return on equity or other accounting criteria.

Quantitative goals in the form of market share or sales volume should always be included. If there are no quantitative goals, the economic goals can be achieved by shrinking the scale of business.

The term qualitative goal refers here to customer-perceived quality. It is becoming increasingly common practice for companies to seek feedback from customers in order to adjust their product and thereby stay competitive.

Management by objectives is an expression that means setting a performance goal for an individual or unit without specifying the means or strategies to be used in reaching the goals. Management by objectives has become increasingly common, partly as a consequence of social trends that have produced more and more individuals with a high level of personal integrity and the ambition to guide their own activities towards set goals. This means that it is sometimes difficult to describe what the goal looks like, because the whole point of management by objectives is that the person closest to the problem is given responsibility for finding his or her way to the goal.

A model has been developed for management by objectives. It assumes that a superior and his subordinate agree on goals for the subordinate's work within a given time frame. Here the superior approaches the subordinate in the guise of a consultant rather than a boss. The formulation of the goal follows roughly the following sequence:

1 The subordinate's present role and duties are taken as the starting point.
2 The subordinate states what goals of his own he wants to reach during the time frame in question.
3 On the basis of the subordinate's present situation and his declared ambitions, the superior and subordinate together try to define a suitable assignment for the latter. It must be so formulated that the subordinate regards it as a challenge that he is capable of accepting.
4 When the subordinate is satisfied with the assignment, he makes an agreement with his superior and the assignment is confirmed.

(Bruzelius & Skärvad, 1982)

Management by objective stands in contrast to direct management or management by order, where subordinates are given exact instructions on how to act in specific situations.

Management by programme means describing in great detail how work is to be done. It involves setting up a number of patterns of repetitive behaviour.

Strategic control is a relatively new management model which I, for one, favour. It means that the responsible manager is not given a completely free hand to set strategies for reaching goals but is required to accept assistance with strategy development that will improve his chances of reaching the set goals.

Mission is a term sometimes used to denote the purpose or *raison d'être* of an activity. It is often applied to a function in a larger business organization, for example 'the mission of the SAS Operations Division'. Complicated hierarchies of goals and ideologies are sometimes constructed in which the word mission is used as a synonym for corporate mission. The terminology of goals is still somewhat imprecise, so caution in the use of the terms is recommended.

INDUSTRY

The meaning of the term industry has broadened from the original sense of manufacturing to include any category of organization that produces goods or services. Thus we can speak of the chemical industry, the tourist industry, the transport industry and the computer software industry.

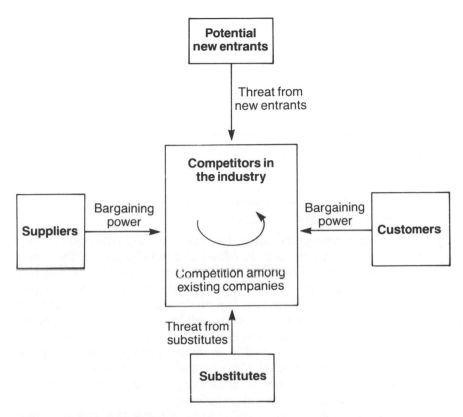

Figure 10 Five competitive forces.

An industry in the broad sense is defined by a number of variables:

1 A specific need, defined by a set of utility functions.
2 Independent decisions by a large number of individuals or organizations concerning purchase of the product or service offered.
3 A common technology developed to satisfy the need.

As long as aero engines were always maintained by the airline that owned the aircraft, aero engine maintenance was not an industry. It only became an industry when a large number of operators began to buy engine maintenance services from independent specialist companies. The same thing has happened with vehicle gearbox manufacture and many other operations in the value-added chain which, as a result of trivialization and specialization, are now bought rather than made by original equipment manufacturers.

Michael Porter has described five competitive forces which operate within an industry (see also Figure 10):

1 Entry of new competitors into the arena.
2 Threat from substitutes based on other technology.
3 Bargaining power of buyers.
4 Bargaining power of suppliers.
5 Competition between companies already established on the market.

Porter's five forces are dealt with in more detail in the third part of this book.

Industries, then, are not static. They rise and decline over a period of time. The definition of the industry is also one of the most important parameters in strategy analysis, for it is the basis of assessment of two key factors:

1 The attractiveness of the industry as such.
2 The company's position within it.

The factors that govern the attractiveness of an industry, growth and profitability, for example, are described in the third part of this book. However, there also seem to be irrational factors that affect the attractiveness of an industry. Some capital owners, for example, are possessed by a desire for intellectual legitimacy that makes the publishing industry attractive to them. Another well-known industry that seems to exert an inexplicable attraction is civil aviation; for years, indeed for decades, it has been unprofitable in many parts of the world, yet people still invest in it. The AGV (Automatic Guided Vehicle) industry is another one that continues to attract capital despite lack of profits, probably because of its technical complexity.

These examples are cited in order to emphasize that the attractiveness of an industry is not determined by objectively determinable criteria alone, but is also influenced by irrationalities such as boyish Biggles dreams, the desire for respectability or blind faith in technology.

The position of a company in its industry is determined by such factors as

1 the market and its movements;
2 profitability compared to competitors;
3 customer-perceived quality;
4 the relative cost positions of various functions within the company.

To recapitulate: an industry is not a static phenomenon, but an evolving one; its attractiveness is influenced by irrational as well as rational factors, and a company's position within its industry is an expression of short-term and long-term businessmanship.

INVESTMENT

Investment means making an economic commitment at the present time in the expectation of receiving revenue in the future. The term investment is traditionally associated with the buying of tangible objects which are capable of generating value for a long time to come and can therefore be listed as assets on the balance sheet.

A term closely linked to investment is DEPRECIATION. It means that the capital committed to an investment remains a charge against the profit-and-loss account for a number of years; the sum invested may for example be distributed over a period of ten years. When one-tenth of an investment is written off every year on the profit-and-loss account, this is called depreciation. Depreciation of inventory is sometimes called write-down.

A couple of points must be clarified to judge the profitability of an investment:

1 How long can the investment be expected to be profitable compared to other possible alternatives (economic lifetime)?
2 What gross margin contribution (revenue less variable costs) will the investment give, and how will the cash flow be distributed over the years to come?

On the basis of these two questions, there are several models for investment calculation, including:

- the present value method, which calculates all cash flows at present value and compares them with the size of the investment
- the payback method, whch calculates the time it will take until the investment has repaid its own cost

The meaning of the term investment has been extended to describe all situations in which an extraordinary present sacrifice is made in the hope of future gains. Market investment is an example of this use of the term. In this context it means spending money on special marketing activities over and above the expenditure on marketing activities normally budgeted to maintain the present volume of sales. This meaning of the word often gets debased, being used to describe any money spent on advertising or sales promotion.

Another use of the term investment relates to know-how and human capital. With growing realization of the importance of human capabilities, people have begun to speak of investing in skills and know-how. Here again it is a matter of an economic commitment made with a view to future gains, although this kind of investment is nearly always booked on the profit-and-loss account, that is, it is shown on the company's books as a straight cost item.

Bad investments can often be disastrous. A new giant shipyard was opened in Uddevalla in Sweden in the mid-1970s at a time when the huge expansion of Japanese and Korean yards was already common knowledge. Investments like the Uddevalla project simply destroy capital.

During the 1960s and 1970s, the countries of Eastern Europe, Poland among them, invested heavily in steelworks, concrete factories and shipyards. In the socialist view, investment in heavy industrial plant is a Good Thing. These investments, made under the Gierek administration, have led to a sharp fall in living standards in Poland and necessitated heavy foreign borrowing that has crippled the country's economic development.

The prevailing culture of the civil aviation industry has prompted investment in new aircraft, preferably big ones, as peer-group status symbols. This is probably one of the reasons why the total profitability of all IATA-affiliated airlines is so low as to be negligible.

Investment in know-how can also turn out badly. The rise of big engineering consultancy firms during the period when Sweden was expanding its infrastructure led to a surplus of engineers, and to economic difficulties for those firms when the expansion phase came to an end.

Bad investments can likewise be made in product development (the Concorde airplane is the classic case of that error of judgment), and in markets (as when several foreign manufacturers of heavy goods vehicles tried to break into a Swedish market dominated by two domestic manufacturers, Volvo and Scania).

Investment decisions are among the most vital decisions that companies make, and need to be taken with great care and the right feel for business.

It is received wisdom that high capital intensity leads to low profitability. There are three main reasons for this:

1 High capital intensity leads to harder competition, especially when sales are sluggish and capacity is not fully utilized. That kind of situation, more than any other, tends to result in price-cutting and market wars.
2 Closing down a manufacturing operation involves such heavy losses that companies tend to struggle on too long.
3 Margin pricing is common in situations of high capital intensity.

We may further note that businesses with a low capital intensity are often more profitable than their more capital-intensive competitors. This applies in cases where competition is hard and fixed assets are not fully utilized. It does not of course apply where manufacturing

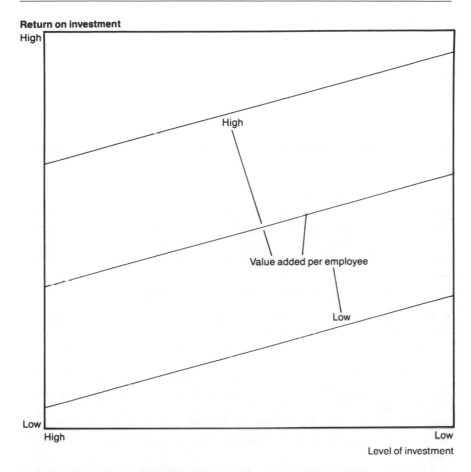

Return on investment

Figure 11 Investment level and returns. The graph illustrates how a high sales value per employee combined with low investment-to-sales ratio gives the highest profitability in terms of return on investment. A high volume of investment and low value added, often synonymous with small margins, typically results in the worst conceivable profitability. A high level of investment reduces profitability, but high productivity can partly offset this.

capacity is utilized to the full, but that condition is rarely fulfilled nowadays.

If a business decides to make a heavy investment in manufacturing capacity, its productivity per employee must be drastically increased to avoid a drop in profitability. Companies with high productivity combined with a low capital-to-turnover ratio may be several times more profitable than others with low productivity and high capital commitment.

The technique of relating tied-up capital to value added offers interesting opportunities for making comparisons between companies, not only in the same industry but also in different industries.

LEADERSHIP

The term leadership has undergone a change of meaning in line with the new philosophy of management by consent instead of by authority. Leadership used to imply the power to issue orders in an organization, whereas now it is exercised with the consent and collaboration of the persons working under the leader.

In modern corporate culture, power is not a remote thing and conditioned obedience is a thing of the past. That is why the concept of leadership is specially important. Once, you could put somebody in charge of an area of responsibility without regard to the feelings or wishes of the people in the organization concerned. You cannot do this today, a fact that has changed the conditions under which leaders operate.

Leadership can be briefly characterized in three points:

1 Giving guidelines for what is to be done.
2 Getting people to co-operate.
3 Supplying the energy needed to reach set goals.

One way to put it is that the foremost duty of a leader is that of continuously adapting, rationalizing and reorienting an enterprise to match its environment. Nowadays we often speak of strategic leadership, which implies the ability to take a long and broad view, and from that perspective to optimize the activities of one's area of responsibility.

Effective communication is one of the principal tools of modern leadership. A leader must attune him or herself to moods and opinions in the organization, and must have the ability to argue persuasively in support of the decisions s/he makes and the course s/he takes.

One might say that modern leadership has become market-oriented in the sense that it proceeds from the need for change in the organization. Starting from need structures improves the odds for successful reorientation. Communication, therefore, is not just a fashionable fad but a useful instrument in situations where impressions must be received and absorbed, leading to new courses of action which must then be forcefully communicated to the outside world.

The following summary, derived from a comprehensive survey, encapsulates the characteristics of a good leader. A good leader is:

• open and extroverted
• inquisitive

- sensitive
- result-oriented
- decisive
- critical
- experimental and tolerant of mistakes
- charismatic
- capable of inspiring confidence and enthusiasm
- calm
- willing to listen
- warm and empathetic
- unfettered by considerations of prestige
- courageous
- unflappable
- flexible
- willing to encourage development in others

It was long assumed that successful leadership in business could be attributed to intelligence, education and analytical ability. Since the reappraisal that took place in the mid–1970s, it has been found that other characteristics contribute strongly to success in business. They include business experience, creativity, drive and holistic vision.

Business experience in this context means having experienced or studied a number of business situations. Creativity means the ability to combine existing elements of knowledge in new, innovative ways. Drive means the ability to proceed from thought to deed without getting entangled in analysis. Holistic vision means both strategic management ability, that is the ability to discern patterns of change, and a talent for striking an optimum balance between customer-perceived value and rational deployment of resources.

Unfortunately, the term leadership as commonly used has come to refer only to 'soft' variables such as ability to arouse enthusiasm and persuade an organization to go along with the leader's ideas. This ignores the aspect of strategic leadership, the ability to assess business situations correctly and make wise strategic decisions.

Most people, when asked whether Adolf Hitler was a good leader, tend to answer in the affirmative. While strongly deprecating his ethics, they perceive him as a highly capable leader. An interesting discussion ensues when they are reminded of the fact that his Thousand Year Reich only lasted for twelve years; the discussion centres around the fact that although he succeeded in getting the German people to follow him, albeit by dubious methods, his chosen strategy proved disastrous even in the medium term.

Analytically, leadership ability and strategic ability are two distinct things. The ability to manage people and the ability to manage a business are not necessarily combined in one person. A leader type assisted by a strategist is an excellent combination, if it can be made to work.

MARKET

A market can be defined as an organized meeting for trade, originally a town square where sellers could find buyers and vice versa.

Today, the term market is an abstraction, a collective term for a group of customers who may be united either by geographical location or by common needs that generate demand. The use of the word market in both these senses often causes confusion, so a more detailed explanation is called for.

In the geographical sense, the term market can for example be applied to a country or region: the Norwegian market or the European market. Here the term is applied to all customers in a given geographical area, regardless of what products they buy or how they use them.

Market segments

Bankers speak of the private market and the company market, and manufacturers of hand tools speak of the DIY (Do-It-Yourself) market and the pro market. The bankers are of course referring to those of their customers who are private individuals and companies respectively, while the toolmakers are talking about people in a geographical area who buy tools for private use in the home and for professional use at work. In these two examples, the term market is really an abbreviation for market segment. A segment is a part of a whole where differences within the part are smaller than differences between that part and other parts.

The use of the term market as an abstraction has sometimes caused large companies to make the mistake of failing to consider individual customers and to learn about their customers' need structures.

If you use the term market as a name for broad categories, you run the risk of blunting your sensitivity to subtle differences in the need structures of your customers.

Market orientation

Market orientation means a view of management based on the market and its needs. By identifying the market's needs, the underlying factors that create demand, a company can adapt its resources (its costs and capital) accordingly and thus make itself more competitive.

The term market orientation has come to be used as a contrast to the older technocratic view, which was based on the company's resources and strengths and which aimed at persuading the market to want what the company had to offer.

Market orientation thus denotes a more entrepreneurial view; it calls for willingness to listen to the customers you want to serve and for empathy, for the ability to put yourself in the other person's place.

Market analysis

Market analysis is the collection, processing and compilation of data that provide information about the market for a company, product or service. A distinction is made between quantitative market analysis, which refers to the collection of data about numbers of buyers, frequency of buying, seasonal variations, and so on, and qualitative market analysis. The latter covers things like attitude polls, surveys of customer-perceived quality and image studies. Image here means reality as perceived by those around one.

Market analysis originated in the consumer goods trade, and its industrial applications are not yet fully developed, but its use among the manufacturing and service industries is now growing rapidly. The growth of the service and software sectors, in particular, has created a growing need for qualitative studies. In large corporations, too, it is becoming increasingly common for departments and sections to measure their performance in serving in-house users of their products and services.

MARKETING

Marketing stands for creation of demand, whereas selling stands for getting orders. In everyday speech the term marketing is used loosely for both processes, for both spreading the word about a product and actually selling it. Marketing is one of the four basic functions of management, together with development, production and administration.

Most industries during the greater part of the twentieth century have experienced a constant rise in demand, which made marketing seem less important than production or administration. The first two decades after World War II, in particular, were marked by a worldwide shortage of goods that made marketing skills superfluous. But the shortages gradually gave way to surpluses, once most needs were satisfied. This resulted in a sharp upswing of interest in marketing in the early 1960s, when both marketers and market communicators became much more important people in the corporate world.

During this period the marketers tried to extend the meaning of the term to cover both market studies and product development, as well as creation of demand and physical distribution of goods. Note that the term marketing is still sometimes used in this sense, with a definition so broad that it tends to dilute the term to the point of meaninglessness. In the interests of clarity in communication, it is advisable to distinguish between product development and marketing.

Creation of demand

Demand is created in radically different ways depending on what kind of product or service you are supplying. If you are selling nuclear power stations, you have little need for mass communications in the form of print advertising in the daily press, a medium which is very important to sales of fast-moving consumer goods like toiletries and groceries. If you are a lawyer or management consultant selling professional services, your efforts to create demand must be adapted to the channels through which buyers are open to influence, specifically by making them aware of highclass work you have already done.

Many people, through ignorance of the meaning of the term marketing, associate it with advertisements in the daily papers. Readers of this glossary are asked to remember that marketing means creation of demand, and that demand is created in many different ways according to what kind of goods or services are being sold, and to whom.

The Nordic School of Service Marketing has developed a model which is described on pages 181–3. It was designed by Grönroos and Gummesson, and its merit lies in its proof of the importance of expectations to customer-perceived quality.

Internal marketing

This is a term that has come into use in recent years to describe measures taken to increase motivation through effective internal communication of a company's visions, goals, corporate mission and strategic course. Many companies have discovered that they can achieve substantial improvements in efficiency by motivating their employees to perform better by putting more of their energy into their work. The employee benefits too, because he comes to regard his work as more meaningful and his whole life as richer. Internal marketing is dealt with in more detail under the heading of COMMUNICATION.

Market investment

This term (see also INVESTMENT) is nowadays used for almost any kind of marketing activity. Advertising agencies, in particular, use market investment as a sales argument, invariably claiming that expenditure on marketing should be regarded as an investment. This is just not true.

An investment is a commitment made at the present time that will yield a return for a long time to come. Thus in a marketing context, the term investment cannot be applied to the regular expenditure on marketing activities that is needed to maintain a budgeted volume of sales. The term market investment ought to be reserved for extraordinary situations in which a major effort is made to penetrate a new market or launch a new product.

Marketing communications

This is a collective name for all activities of an informative nature intended to persuade customers to ask for and buy a company's product (goods and/or services). Marketing communication is usually distinguished from other kinds of communication because it calls for special skills.

The term marketing communication is used mainly by advertising agencies, but they cannot always be expected to be fully informed about what kind of marketing communication is best suited to a company's needs. They often have a strong tendency to lean towards advertising in the daily and trade press. The true meaning of marketing communication covers all kinds of communication activities. So be careful how you use the term.

The model illustrated in Figure 12 is often used to visualize three phenomena:

1 The proportion of customers who know about a product.
2 The proportion of the total market and of those who know about the product who have tried it.
3 The proportion who make repeat purchases, which is a credible confirmation that the supplier has satisfied the customers' needs.

MARKET SHARE

The importance of market share has long been acknowledged, especially in traditional strategic thinking. Relative market share, above all, has been the focus of attention. This is because a high relative market share was believed to offer opportunities for mass production with consequent economies of scale. These economies in turn would mean long runs, low unit costs, high margins and high profitability. The theory was based on the Experience Curve invented by the commanding officer of the Wright Patterson US Army Air Force base in

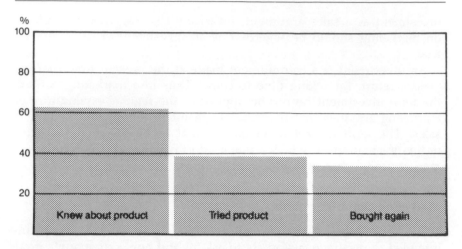

%

Figure 12 Test of efficiency of marketing. In this case, 63 per cent of consumers knew about the product, 39 per cent had tried it and 33 per cent had bought it more than once.

Dayton, Ohio in 1926. He discovered that unit costs fell by about 20 per cent every time production was doubled. This correlation, which applies to manufacture of physical products, later came to dominate strategic thinking and also influenced theories about market shares (*see* the EXPERIENCE CURVE model).

The value of theories on market share has since been called into question. A large market share is something that cannot be achieved simply by investing in expansion. Still less can a sustained high market share be gained by acquisition. The only way to get a high market share is to earn it, that is by satisfying customers' needs so well that enough of them prefer your product to give you a high market share compared to your competitors.

Sometimes the theory works admirably, but sometimes it gives totally wrong answers. It all depends on the material from which market share is measured. The term can only be meaningful if you define the market in which your company wants to stake a claim, and which is significant to the outcome of competition. This is known as the market served. If you manufacture concrete beams for private houses, the market served will be fairly small, maybe within a radius of 150 km from your factory. If on the other hand you build airliners or nuclear power stations, your market served is global in extent.

A strong emphasis on a large market share is often justified. It must however be remembered that the conception of the importance of market share originated in the United States, where competitive strategy is heavily focused on rational production and price. Europe, on the other hand, has traditionally attached more importance to segmentation and quality. In a fragmented market with no advantages of scale and a low level of awareness of available alternatives among buyers, market share is relatively unimportant.

Conversely, market share becomes much more important in concentrated markets with substantial advantages of scale and with knowledgeable customers. The British automotive industry, for example, committed a serious error of judgement by persisting in measuring its market share relative to the British market. By failing to redefine the market it served, it lost sight of potential advantages of scale in both production and, later, development.

MOTIVATION

Motivation, to put it briefly, is what makes an individual act and behave in a certain way. It is a combination of intellectual, physiological and psychological processes that decides, in a given situation, how vigorously you act and in what direction your energy is channelled.

There are innumerable classifications of human motives. The reason why motives are so interesting is that they are actually a synonym for needs. Motives and needs, in their turn, provide the basic key to all organized activity, especially business activity.

In his book *Psykologi och arbetsorganisationen* (Psychology and Work Organization) Sven Söderberg cites a classification made by the Danish psychologist K. B. Madsen. Madsen distinguished nineteen basic motives, which he divided into four groups:

1 Organic motives:
   1 hunger
   2 thirst
   3 sex urge
   4 maternal urge
   5 avoidance of pain
   6 avoidance of cold (self-protection)
   7 avoidance of heat
   8 anal urge (excretion)
   9 urge to breathe

2 Emotional motives:
   10 fear or security motive
   11 aggression or combative motive

3 Social motives:
   12 desire for contact

13 desire for power (self-assertion)
14 desire to perform

4 Activity motives:
  15 need for experience
  16 need for physical action
  17 curiosity (intellectual activity)
  18 need for excitement (emotional activity)
  19 creative urge (complex activity)

The way people act, their buying behaviour for example, is generally controlled by a number of simultaneously acting motivational forces. Motive systems thus arise which are a complex of different motives that in their turn control a certain pattern of behaviour. When motive systems block each other or are mutually opposed, we speak of conflicting motives.

Individual variations in areas of interest are an expression of motive systems. They may comprise physical action, curiosity, excitement, or experience in general and creative activity.

The performance, power and contact motives are others that often occur in motive systems. All the components of a motive system are important to the performance of a certain action, a job of work, for example. It is therefore to the benefit of both the individual, his employer and society at large if he takes an interest in his work. Interest is a powerful driving force, a motive system in itself, in fact. Madsen puts it like this:

1 It is important that the activity motive gets maximum satisfaction from work. In any work situation it is possible to create variation in order to satisfy the motives of physical action, excitement and curiosity.
2 It is also important to satisfy the performance motive. As Frederick Taylor, the American management theorist, once expressed it, it is a matter of putting the right person in the right place, so that every individual feels he is exercising his or her powers to the full.
3 Finally, it is important to satisfy the contact motive. If this is not possible in the actual work situation, opportunities for leisure-time contact must be provided.

The social motives, specifically the performance motive, are present in all of us in varying degrees. Suppose that you could enhance the performance motive in an organization just a little: it would result in a substantial boost to that organization's charge of energy, for social motives can be influenced. They are strongly affected by the environ-

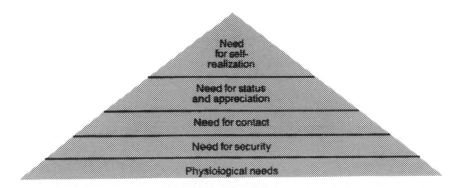

Figure 13 Maslow's five-level pyramid of needs. Many research workers and practitioners have emphasized the necessity of understanding the behaviour of individuals.

ment in which we find ourselves and the things that inspire our confidence.

David McClelland has been engaged in research since the end of the 1940s, and has provided us with plenty of useful practical knowledge and methods relating to entrepreneurship, methods for measuring and developing entrepreneurial qualities in people.

Many researchers and practitioners have pointed out how essential it is to understand the driving forces that account for an individual's behaviour. This applies within the framework of a work organization, in which the motives of the individual should ideally match the work he is set to do. It applies even more to how well the management of a company understands the motive systems of the customers their company serves. Motive systems are the true criteria for segmentation, a term which means the division of a population into subgroups characterized by similar motive systems.

Well-known names in motivational research are Abraham Maslow, Frederick Herzberg and Victor H. Vroom. It is the last-named who has most strongly underlined the importance of relating an individual's motivation and acts to the goals of the organization and of the individual himself. If we understand these relationships, we will also understand why an individual acts in a certain way instead of several other possible ways.

NEEDS

Needs are an expression of underlying motives that control demand. Thus need and demand are not the same thing. Let us take an example. All human beings have a need to feel successful. That is why people often prefer to reduce their burden of responsibility to a load that they can handle successfully rather than keep on carrying more responsibility that they feel is too much for them.

One way to satisfy the need for success is to display symbols of success. For a company executive, this may mean acquiring a turbo-charged car or a personal computer. In this case the underlying need is the desire to feel and display success, whereas the demand can take a variety of forms.

Needs in the most widely differing contexts can likewise express themselves in different ways. The need of a businessman to feel successful by heading a profitable company can express itself in a business development programme, a planned reduction of costs or of tied-up capital through inventory cutback, a reduction of receivables or the sale of some fixed asset.

Discussions of need and demand are apt to get complicated. There are two main reasons for this:

1 Many people do not know the difference between need and demand.
2 It is important to enter the hierarchy of needs at the right level, the one that is relevant to what you want to talk about.

The latter point may seem somewhat cryptic, but if for example we talk about the needs that an air freight service satisfies, it is enough to address the buyers' needs for rational transport to improve the profitability of their own operations. It is unnecessary to go to the level of a chief executive's need to feel successful by running a success-ful business. That level is irrelevant to the situation in hand.

Needs are very often designated by the expression *utility functions*. Total customer utility can be broken down into a number of utility functions, which in turn can be evaluated against each other both for a total market and for parts of that market. In the latter case this gives input for segmentation, i.e. division of a total population into groups with shared value judgements concerning utility functions.

All business is based on short-term and long-term efficiency. Efficiency is defined as value to the customer in relation to pro-ductivity. Value is the quotient between customer utility and price, while productivity is the quotient between number of units produced and cost. The efficiency of a business is thus expressed by the quotient between value and productivity; this explains the importance of utility functions.

One problem with needs is that the relevant need structures change with time. The word 'relevant' above refers to the needs that are crucial in a business situation. Back in the 1960s safety was an argu-ment relevant to the choice of a car. In the late 1980s it is no longer relevant, because all cars are seen as pretty much equal in terms of safety. The motor trade's analysts long assumed that we motorists chose our cars on the basis of a rational trade off between price and performance. That was why mass production, the 'world car' and cheap cars were the predominant strategic themes throughout the 1970s. The rational man's weakness is that he tends to ignore the psychological shadings of need structures, and thus falls into the rationality trap.

The airline industry offers another illustrative example of the importance of identifying the right level in the hierarchy of needs. Business travellers have a rational need for business communication, and perhaps an irrational need to get away from the daily grind and see something else for a change. With regard to the need for communication, substitutes are gradually beginning to appear that will have significant effects on the future development of the industry. Communication by images, or video conferences, is likely to come into increasing demand as a solution to the need to communicate. Image communication is superior to air travel in that it saves time, does not cause jet lag, etc.; on the other hand it does not satisfy the irrational need to get away from it all which is sometimes combined with the rational need for business communication. The question then arises of which level of the hierarchy of needs should be chosen for the purpose of defining corporate mission, etc.

An understanding of how need influences demand is a fundamental and necessary ability in business. If the consumer co-operative movement fails to realize that shopping for groceries ought to be a pleasant experience that satisfies a need for entertainment, its prospects of capturing new market shares will be poor. If it has also fallen into the rationality trap of believing that people look only at price and performance and accordingly puts anonymous products on its shelves, it has further demonstrated its failure to understand essential aspects of customers' needs. Another example: a large company selling complicated mechanical equipment had neglected its customers' legitimate need for good after-sales service in the form of spare parts and technical service at reasonable prices and with quick delivery.

An area of need must be broken down into utility functions to identify all the variables that add up to customer-perceived quality.

Modern, entrepreneurial management is characterized by a strong and genuine interest in the need structures that control customer demand. That is where the key to successful businessmanship often lies.

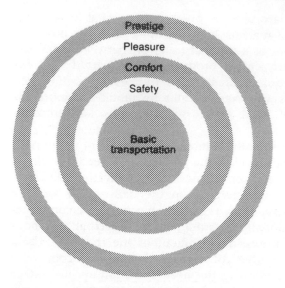

Figure 14 Our actions are controlled by our needs. A car satisfies different needs, as the figure illustrates.

OPTIMIZATION – OPERATIONS ANALYSIS

Optimization is a frequently used term in the field of strategy. It is usually defined in one of the following two ways:

1 Getting something to work as well as possible by balancing the various factors involved.
2 A technique for calculating the best allocation of resources for a given purpose within given constraints.

Theories of optimization underwent rapid development during World War II, when the problem was to transport huge quantities of personnel and equipment over vast distances. The result was a series of techniques collectively known as operations analysis.

Operations analysis is defined as an interdisciplinary expertise in quantifying various aspects of a problem complex, and using mathematical models to verify and optimize the situation. It includes a variety of techniques such as:

- linear programming
- PERT
- decision trees
- Monte Carlo simulation
- queuing theory
- critical paths
- regression models

The strength of optimization lies in its ability to achieve the best possible situation in given circumstances. What optimization cannot do, however, is change the circumstances. It thus lends itself admirably to application in stable situations where the object is to achieve a high degree of efficiency in production or distribution.

The demand variable in optimization models is usually determined by forecasting. All experience to date shows that forecasts are unreliable. As a result, optimizations have often been worthless because one of the key input parameters was often uncertain or wrong.

For a long time after World War II, problems of strategy almost always involved a choice between growth alternatives. A forecast formed the basis of the optimization, which was made with the help of operations analysis techniques. This led in turn to demands for procurement and allocation of resources, which nearly always consisted exclusively of costs and capital. The operations analysis approach acquired a bad reputation that it did not altogether deserve because the techniques were often used in a way that revealed a total lack of business sense on the part of the people who applied them.

Suboptimization is a good example of misapplication. This term refers to the best alternative in given circumstances within an area that is part of a greater whole. In everyday language the word suboptimization is used to mean a course of action that is judged to be inappropriate and wrong and which shows no understanding of the wider perspective. Let me illustrate with a few telling examples from the pen of Göran Albinsson Bruhner:

> Suboptimization means optimization, i.e. best possible fulfilment, of a *subordinate* purpose. The point is that by attempting to optimize a subordinate objective, one may come into conflict with *overall* optimization.
>
> A typical case of unwise suboptimization is a Municipal Highways Department's decision to save money by cutting down on pavement sanding in wintertime, because the economic calculations take no account of the extra costs for broken arms and legs. These costs are paid for by the National Insurance, and ultimately by the taxpayer. So what the local authority saves its residents in maintenance costs, they have to pay several times over for medical treatment.
>
> Ill-considered suboptimization is common in the public sector, where the left hand often does not know – or care – what the right hand is doing. The latest insanity of this kind in Sweden is the decision to save public money by closing down geriatric and psychiatric hospitals. This is particularly cruel, because the helpless patients involved must pay a heavy price in suffering.

Suboptimization is of course a problem in business too. Decisions that make good sense from a departmental point of view do not necessarily benefit the company as a whole.

A common conflict of optimization is the one between inventory and sales. Keeping a large and varied selection of products in stock is expensive, but also helps to increase the volume of sales. The company loses if it accepts suboptimization of either inventory or sales; total optimization demands a compromise between the two conflicting claims.

We can also speak of suboptimization in the time dimension. In the short term it may seem most advantageous not to invest in new buildings, new machinery or product development, whereas failure to do so may turn out to be far from advantageous – disastrous in fact – in the long run. Companies that refuse to worry about the future often have no future to worry about.

Decentralization is the catchword today in both business and public administration. As always when new fashions catch on, persuasion takes precedence over reflection. I strongly suspect that the dangers of suboptimization are being overlooked in the general enthusiasm for decentralization.

(Bruhner 1991)

ORGANIC GROWTH

By analogy with the chain structure of carbon atoms in organic molecules, the term organic growth has been adopted in the business world to mean expansion based on an existing corporate structure, as distinct from expansion by diversification or acquisition.

Generally speaking, there are three ways for a company to grow:

1 Organic growth as described here.
2 Acquisition of companies or business units which are parts of companies.
3 Branching out into other lines of business (diversification).

For the businessman or woman, the ability to grow organically is always evidence of strength, because it is proof of their ability to improve business. A company that develops successfully from the base of its own resources has proved that it is competitive, that customers prefer its products to its competitors'. This assumes that its growth rate has exceeded that of the market, meaning that it has captured market shares.

Often, however, managements find the process of organic growth too slow, and try to speed it up by buying companies. This is a risky business, as the odds against success are high. The most important thing to bear in mind in this context, however, is that the risk of failure in acquisition rises sharply if your own business is not already growing. Business development capability, documented by organic growth of various kinds, is a valuable insurance premium in connection with acquisitions.

Take the example of the Volvo Car Corporation's acquisition of DAF, which was made from a position of weakness. It was not an economic success. It can be contrasted with the Volvo Truck Corporation's acquisition of White in the United States, or its deal with General Motors. Though these were long-term acquisitions, they have already begun to show promising results. They were made from a position of strength based on good organic growth.

Growth based on in-house resources is even more important in the software industries. Acquisitions in those industries are related to assets in the form of human knowledge, and such assets are not fixed; they can get up and leave.

One example of organic growth is SAS's development of catering into a separate business unit, Service Partner. Many accountancy firms have branched out into tax counselling and consultancy, mainly in the area of financial control. Saab used its experience in military aviation to build passenger planes.

Two boundary lines for organic growth can be clearly stated:

1 The term organic growth is used in contrast to growth by acquisition, that is by buying other companies or shares in them.
2 The term organic growth is also used in contrast to ventures into new types of business unrelated to a company's basic operations.

PORTFOLIO

The most usual meaning of the term portfolio in a business context is the collection of securities that one owns. By extension, the term has also come to mean a group of business units. It derives from the term share portfolio, which refers to a stock market investment comprising shares of a number of different companies.

By analogy, the term portfolio as used in business has come to mean a more or less variegated group of business units under the same ownership, together constituting what in legal parlance is called a group of companies. Other common terms are a corporation, concern or conglomerate.

A portfolio can come into being in many ways. Sometimes a new corporate mission arises out of an auxiliary function, as when Service Partner grew out of SAS's catering service.

Other business porfolios are the offspring of a customer-supplier relationship; this is also called VERTICAL INTEGRATION. A shipyard may buy a steelworks to make its structural steel (backward integration), or it may buy a banana plantation or a coal company to secure cargoes for its ships (forward integration). A car manufacturer may buy a chain of dealerships or the factory that makes its back axles. An airline may buy into the travel agency business, maintain its own engines and operate hotels.

Yet another way in which porfolios can arise is through development of related businesses to meet customers' needs better. In the data consultancy business, groups of business units have developed in symbiosis (sharing of a common habitat for mutual benefit by organisms of different kinds), each satisfying one kind of need and thus finding more ways to reach customers.

A portfolio may thus be either diversified or synergistic. Intermediate forms also exist, of course. In good times there is a tendency to overrate synergies and cite them as a motive for acquisitions, even though the true motives may be quite different.

Portfolios often become diversified because synergies, with time, grow diffuse and eventually meaningless. This means that a change in ownership may have to be considered. A common pattern is that a portfolio which has grown up on a basis of synergies in production gradually loses its synergistic connections. Market relations become more essential, creating an entirely different business situation.

Managing and developing a portfolio is a matter of working with business structures rather than business strategies. The chief executive of a company or corporation that contains a large number of diverse business units is in fact in the business unit industry. Since a company almost always contains more than one business unit, its management must be able to:

- buy into new industries
- strengthen business units, for example by acquisition
- withdraw from unwanted industries
- sell business units that can be better managed by others
- allocate resources in the form of capital and costs
- ensure that individual business units are strategically managed
- take advantage of synergies in the form of greater business strength or more efficient operative management of business units

When a company consists of several units with little or no synergy, discussions of corporate mission are apt to be long and complicated. Some thinkers have dubbed an intermediate form 'business areas', by which they mean synergistic porfolios where market synergies or similarities of customers' needs make it possible to find some sort of common trade logic.

If you are managing a porfolio that consists of a number of business units with different corporate missions, one of your main problems will be that of dismantling structures that do not fit. Entrepreneurial managers will disinvest without a qualm, but power-oriented managers seem to have a hangup about selling business units.

There are of course logical and justifiable reasons for the existence of porfolios of disparate business units. These reasons include:

1 The dynamics of the business have generated organic growth, as in the case of Service Partner in SAS or the Volvo Bus Corporation in the Volvo Group.
2 Technological skills have led to the development of business areas related to the original one only by technology.
3 The main business area has been highly profitable but offered no opportunities for new investment.
4 It is desirable to spread business risks.
5 Strong links exist between business units in terms of customer needs or technology.
6 Costs or capital structures can be shared.

Mixtures of legal structure (companies or units with the same owner) and business structure often occur. It is important for businessmen in general and readers of this book in particular to recognize the difference between legal and business structures.

POSITIONING

The term positioning has become increasingly popular. It has its origins in advertising agency jargon, and its meaning lies in the boundary zone between marketing, portfolio strategy and business strategy. On occasions, it has played an important part in focusing the resources of a corporation and thereby guiding its strategic course. The examples of Volkswagen in the United States (Small is Beautiful) and of Long Island Trust, which successfully positioned itself as the bank for Long Islanders, show how positioning can help to attain a strategic focus and lead to success.

The purpose of positioning is:

- to make a company's capabilities known
- to improve performance
- to explain a many-faceted whole with organic links
- to secure a given place for the product in the minds of all concerned

Positioning is thus primarily a matter of changing attitudes, and only secondarily of changing the product.

Positioning further implies a comparative rather than superlative form of expression. The company and its products are related to the world around them, for example to competitors or to other products on the market. The idea is not to ascribe superlative qualities to the product which strain credulity and acceptance.

I have already mentioned how Volkswagen positioned itself on the American small-car market. The Volkswagen Beetle was viewed as a small car, a position which was deliberately affirmed by the succinct message 'Small is Beautiful'. By establishing itself in the public mind as the strongest contender on the small-car market, it automatically gave its marketing a boost.

Another aspect of positioning is that it reinforces attitudes already held by the public. The object is not to change attitudes, but to conjure up latent associations. You can do this, for example, by making it clear what you are not; 'Seven-up, the non-cola'.

Positioning, then, involves manipulating mental associations. The trick is to find a window in the consciousness and latch on to something that is already there, to reinforce rather than create by confirming associations.

Positioning is most nearly related to the concept of image, which means the way the public perceives reality, and is an expression of customer-perceived quality, of the way a company is viewed in the light of a number of need-related variables.

Positioning is also a way of achieving distinction, of staking a claim to be best in some particular segment, that is in a sub-set of a need area or of a total market.

To sum up:

- positioning is a planned method of finding a way into the public consciousness
- concentrate on the recipient of the message: how will the customer react to your message and your offer?
- associate with what is already in people's minds
- keep the message simple
- the easiest and best positioning technique is to be first to occupy a position
- a position once taken must be consistently and persistently held
- an anti-position (what we are not) is often easy to communicate
- never try to position yourself head-on to the market leader
- the main object of a positioning programme should be to strive for leadership in a defined area
- find a hole in the market: is there a vacant position anywhere?

The idea of positioning is not, of course, the answer to all problems of communication or strategy. In some cases, however, it can be an excellent aid to thinking. In the first place, you can privately consider the question of what position your company and its products occupy in the minds of your market. In the second place, in some cases, you can use positioning terminology as a focal point for choosing your strategy and achieving a competitive edge. The term positioning merits a prominent place in modern management thinking alongside others like customer-perceived quality and need orientation of the product.

PRICE

Price is defined as a 'predetermined payment for a certain perform-ance' or a 'cost to be paid in the event of purchase'. Price is one of the fundamental variables of businessmanship in that it is an expression of the sacrifice the customer must make to get the utility that a product or service represents.

Historically, price has played a key part in theorization. The Price Theory treats the significance of price in terms of demand, ignoring the value variable on the assumption that products have equal value.

During the post-war period up to the mid-1970s, price adjustments were made rather callously. Little attention was paid to how price related to value given, because most industries were supplying excess demand or, to put it the other way round, because there was a general shortage of goods. In most cases, prices were increased as soon as costs went up.

An imbalance prevailed in many European countries in the second half of the 1970s, in the sense that utility, generally speaking, did not match price levels. As a result of rates of exchange and cost levels pushed sky-high by massive wage increases, prices had reached a level where those countries were losing market shares on the world market. You might say that customers did not feel they were getting utility for the money they were expected to pay. Many companies were then forced to start rethinking their policy of automatically raising prices whenever their costs increased.

For many years, up to about the mid-1970s, organizations regularly compensated their cost increases with price increases. It is possible to do this:

- when competition pressure is low
- when demand exceeds supply
- when you enjoy a position of virtual monopoly

In the situation that has prevailed since the second half of the 1970s, it has been necessary to handle the price instrument with much greater delicacy. Some companies began at an early stage to use price as an instrument of control in the implementation of their strategies (*see* below under *price elasticity of demand*).

In a strategic context, a decisive importance has always been ascribed to price ever since the discovery of the EXPERIENCE CURVE, which says that unit costs fall by about 20 per cent every time output is doubled. Many parallels have been drawn from this correlation in various situations. One example is the thesis that a large market share makes mass production possible at low cost, which in turn makes it possible to cut prices and thereby gain more competitive power.

A cost is what a company actually spends, at the time or over a period of time, on producing a given article or service.

A price is the stipulated sacrifice a customer must make to get the article or service he wants. The price, multiplied by the number of units sold, must in the long term cover costs and yield a return on capital. If the price is related to the value of the product, and if that value is high, the profit can be substantial.

If you look worldwide, you will find that the relationship between the price of an article or service and its utility is not constant. In the United States, for example, price is regarded as more important in relation to utility than it is in Europe. It is not a coincidence that nearly all car-makers in the exclusive car segment are to be found in Europe. This category includes Mercedes, Volvo, Saab, BMW, Audi and Jaguar.

Air travel offers another example where high quality in the form of service or whatever is more important than price to people living in economies with a high standard of living and a high growth rate.

Price sensitivity is well-illustrated by the events of the Gulf War and the recession of 1991. Sensitivity to utility functions in the form of service, etc., diminished in favour of price. People simply changed their position on the Value Graph to strike a different balance between utility and price. The importance of price in the context of travel is also undergoing a long-term change in Europe, where the civil aviation industry, like many others, is in the throes of deregulation.

Price sensitivity is an expression of the extent to which consumers switch suppliers in reaction to a change in prices. Price elasticity of demand, on the other hand, is a measure of changes in total consumption (see below). Airline deregulation and market fluctuations offer good illustrations of both price sensitivity and price elasticity.

Price differentiation is the technique of charging different or variable prices according to what customers are willing to pay. Their willingness to pay depends in turn on their respective need structures and the demands arising therefrom.

Price elasticity of demand measures how the volume of demand is altered by a change in the price of an article or service. It is defined by the following formula:

$$\frac{\text{Percentage change in volume of demand}}{\text{Percentage change in price}}$$

Price elasticity is always expressed as a positive number. When the percentage change in volume of demand is less than the percentage change in price, elasticity is smaller than 1 and demand is said to be inelastic. When the percentage change in volume of demand is more than the percentage change in price, elasticity is larger than 1 and demand is said to be elastic. A demand curve does not normally have the same degree of elasticity along its whole length.

Price elasticity of demand is an essential factor in the formulation of company pricing policies, because volume multiplied by price determines the seller's total gross earnings. If demand is elastic, total earnings increase when prices are cut, whereas a price increase reduces total earnings. Conversely, if demand is inelastic, total earnings rise and fall with prices.

This correlation, on which the economic reasoning of Price Theory is based, is very important in connection with business strategy decisions. Some pioneering work with price elasticity has been done in the airline industry with price cuts that led to recovery of passenger volumes.

Attempts have been made at many times in many places to divorce price from the underlying cost structure and from customers' scales of value. The trouble with this is that the strength of the underlying needs that govern demand can never be measured. One example is the cost of medical care in Scandinavia, where prices have been set so low that demand seems infinite. Other examples can be found in Eastern Europe, where price structures have been distorted by arbitrary political motives.

We can imagine three frames of reference, all of them important, as a basis for pricing:

1 The cost base is used to calculate the lowest price we must charge to operate at a profit.
2 Value to the customer is based on how much customers are prepared to pay for a given utility function.
3 Competitors' prices often determine the level of prices which it is possible and necessary to charge.

To sum up, we can say that price as an instrument of business has become more important now that businessmen have begun to weigh customer-perceived value more carefully against the customer's sacrifice in the form of the price he pays.

PRODUCTIVITY

Productivity in its simplest form can be defined as the number of units of output per unit of input. The simplest formula for measuring profitability is:

$$\text{Man-hour productivity} = \frac{\text{Number of units produced}}{\text{Number of hours worked}}$$

Measurement of productivity in man-hours, however, does not make allowances for input of other resources like materials and capital. In fact the concept of productivity is much more intricate and many-faceted than it appears at first sight.

On a high level of abstraction, all the experts agree that:

$$\text{Productivity} = \frac{\text{Output}}{\text{Input}}$$

But on a more basic level, opinions differ widely about how to define and measure input and output. Man-hour productivity is simplified to the bare bones of how much work workers do per unit of time, with the result that measures intended to increase productivity have often simply led to an acceleration of the pace of work without regard to capital structure or anything else.

Total productivity is a measurement that takes account of all the resources consumed in production: capital, labour and materials. To be able to compare these various resources, input of all of them must be expressed in terms of money or a common standard of value. Labour is naturally an important component of productivity in this wider sense, but the chief significance of total productivity is that internal utilization of resources is combined with the value placed by the market on what is produced. It thus embraces both internal and external productivity, that is both utilization of available resources and the creation of value to customers in some form.

To achieve total productivity we must aim for the top right-hand square of the figure: not only must we produce efficiently, at low cost, but we must also produce the right goods or services. The market determines what the right output is, as well as the value placed on the output in the form of a price per unit. Production, by definition, is based on economic criteria.

There is a strong correlation between productivity and profitability. The profitability of a company depends not only on how efficiently it produces its goods or services, but also to a high degree on what it produces.

The market has to pay a price corresponding to the value which the goods or services represent to the buyer. This price is a direct

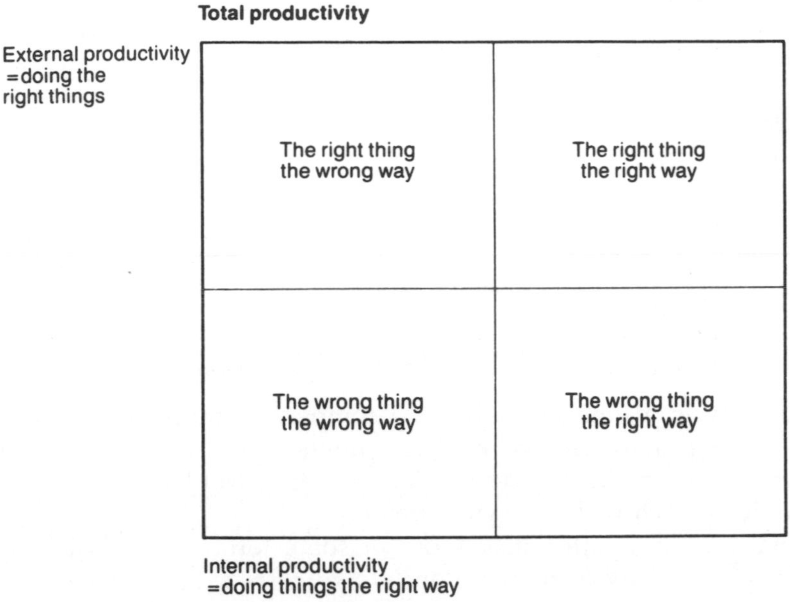

Total productivity

External productivity =doing the right things		
	The right thing the wrong way	The right thing the right way
	The wrong thing the wrong way	The wrong thing the right way

Internal productivity
=doing things the right way

Figure 15 Total productivity.

expression of external productivity, which is thus determined by customers' needs and demand, and not by the work that the organization does.

The total productivity of a company can be described as the quotient between the value generated in the company and the total resources consumed to generate that value. This balances internal use of resources against market-controlled generation of value.

The term efficiency is often used as a synonym for total productivity. When these terms are used, it is very important to recognize their full implications.

Capital productivity is measured as the ratio of units produced to the market value of the total assets required to produce them.

Value-added productivity is a term often used in strategy in comparisons between business units. Value-added productivity is a quotient derived from value added and the number of hours worked, or sometimes the number of persons employed. It is defined as the difference between the value of what is produced and the cost of the purchased materials. This difference is equal to the sum of the contribution to labour and capital, plus profit if any or minus loss if any:

$$\text{Value-added productivity} = \frac{\text{Production value} - \text{Buy-in cost}}{\text{Number of hours worked}}$$

If you change the number of employees by buying products or services from outside, the denominator in the formula changes, but this is matched by a reduction in the numerator because the buy-in cost rises. Changes in value-added productivity are thus an important parameter in make-or-buy analyses.

Another comment concerns the ratio of capital to labour. Investment in automation, for example, reduces both the numerator and the denominator, since interest costs and depreciation rise in the former while input of labour is reduced in the latter. The following modified formula makes these relationships clearer:

$$\text{Value-added productivity} = \frac{\text{Revenue} - (\text{Buy-in} + \text{overhead} + \text{interest} + \text{depreciation}}{\text{Number of hours worked}}$$

Productivity in a functional unit of a company is measured by some criterion of production like invoices, hours flown or units sold in relation to man-hours or payroll. Note that the term has a number of applications, each with its own definition.

Strategy analysis often makes use of some form of expression for relative productivity to compare one's own costs with one's competitors'.

A company is well advised to establish uniform definitions of the terms productivity and efficiency for departments or units to be assessed. If you do a thorough job on this and arrive at agreed criteria, you will be able to make comparisons over a period of time, and perhaps also comparisons with your competitors (*see* Benchmarking).

Definition of value added and profit:

- + sales value (revenue from sales)
- − input costs (cost of current consumption of raw materials, semi-finished goods, energy, transportation and so on)
- = value added (which can be related to the number of persons and/ or the capital employed in the company)
- − personnel costs (wages and salaries paid plus social welfare charges)
- = gross profit (surplus to cover company's fixed costs and return on shareholders' investment).

PRODUCT LIFE CYCLE

Product life cycle is one of the most widely used models for analysis of the successive stages in the development of a business activity, a line of products or an individual product. It is usually visualized as a sales curve extending in time from the date of launch until the product is taken off the market. The product life cycle is usually divided into five phases:

1 Launch.
2 Early growth.
3 Late growth.
4 Maturity.
5 Decline.

The usual explanation of the product cycle is that it originates with an innovation. During the launch phase the management works hard and purposefully to make potential customers aware of the product's competitive advantages, but reaches only a few of the potential customers. Gradually others become interested, and sales take off at an accelerating rate. The product is now in its early growth phase.

In the late growth phase, sales continue to increase, but at a slower rate. Eventually the product reaches maturity, a plateau where the growth rate slows to zero and the volume of sales is dictated by the need for replacements. Finally new substitute products begin to appear on the market, attracting customers away from the existing product, and sales begin to fall off. The decline continues until production is discontinued.

The product life cycle has explanatory value in many contexts. It has played a large part in strategy analysis in many companies, but has latterly tended to be replaced by more sophisticated models.

PROFITABILITY

The term profitability is generally used as a synonym for return on investment (ROI), the earnings generated by capital invested in a business. Return on investment is calculated by the formula:

$$ROI = \frac{Revenues - Costs}{Capital}$$

ROI, however, is meaningless as a criterion of the profitability of heavily software-oriented companies. The return on capital invested in, say, a data consultancy firm says very little about that firm's performance, because the substantial capital generally consists of the office furniture, computers, and possibly company cars. In assessing the profitability of companies that produce services, we must use other yardsticks like profit margin, that is the ratio of profit to turnover, or some other appropriate criterion.

The ROI formula does however apply to companies that depend on capital invested in fixed assets and/or inventory to carry on their

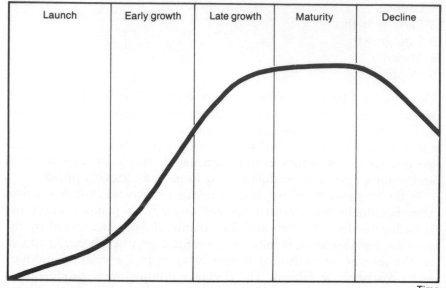

Figure 16 Product life cycle: the five phases in the life cycle of a product, from launch to phase-out. When the product has reached the maturity phase, sales stop growing and a plateau is reached where the need for replacements determines the volume of sales. Eventually new products appear to compete with the existing one, and sales fall off.

business. A holistic view of business management generally involves the ability to manipulate all the components of the ROI formula:

1 Revenues are simply price times quantity, whether you are selling goods or services. The price you can charge depends on customer-perceived value; marketing skills determine what quantity you can sell.
2 Costs are of two kinds. The first are fixed or capacity costs, which remain the same no matter how many or how few units you manufacture or sell. The second are variable or unit costs, which are incurred only when units are manufactured and sold.
3 Capital consists of fixed assets, receivables and inventory. Capital is interesting because it occurs in both the numerator and the denominator of the ROI formula, appearing in the numerator as interest and depreciation costs. The effects of a reduction in capital are therefore considerable.

Although it is quite easy in theory to calculate the major effects of capital rationalization on profitability, knowledge of the practical art of capital rationalization is fairly new. It is only in recent years that managements have begun to use capital as an active means of improving profitability.

A key question that has yet to find a theoretical answer is how to judge the profitability of non-financial capital such as individual skills and know-how. There are service companies that depend on both non-financial and financial capital.

The book *Den Osynliga Balansräkningen* (*The Invisible Balance Sheet*), published in Sweden by Affärsvärldens förlag, proposes a number of new key indicators for accounting, control and evaluation of know-how companies. Several public consultancy companies have begun to use the new indicators in their annual reports.

Strategy development aims at long-term profitability, while operative management aims at short-term profitability. Time frame is a key question in business management. What sacrifices do we need to make today to assure future profitability? Long-term development of a strategic nature is almost always booked as a cost, reducing the profit recorded in the year-end accounts. Yet the return on such investments takes a long time to become apparent. A holistic leader naturally strives for both short-term and long-term profitability, though the latter may conflict with his emoluments, career prospects, etc. Setting the time frame for profitability is a tough problem.

QUALITY

The concept of quality has grown in importance in recent times. The reason is that quality has become a more significant factor in competition in situations where supply exceeds demand. You can sell practically any kind of goods, even shoddy ones, in an expanding market where demand is high. The situation has changed radically since the mid-1970s, and the quality of goods and services has grown more and more important to competitive ability.

Quality is one of the newly discovered factors that have proved to be of decisive significance for success in business.

Originally, quality was measured in terms of number of defects, a measure of the number of faults per unit produced. The term functional quality, which came into use later, meant that products were assessed in terms of their ability to perform the function the customer wanted to use them for. And when we speak of quality today, we mean customer-perceived quality. This includes all the factors that influence a customer's choice of supplier, and thus represents a substantial broadening of the meaning of the term in the direction of value.

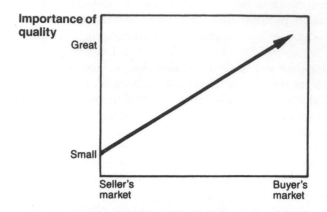

Figure 17 Importance of quality. Quality becomes more important as the market balance shifts from excess demand to excess supply.

PIMS (PROFIT IMPACT OF MARKETING STRATEGY is an instrument for strategy analysis based on data from nearly 3,000 business units. These units were described in terms of more than 30 variables, of which customer-perceived quality was one. The interesting thing about PIMS is that it gives opportunities for research on the importance of individual variables to success in business. It has been found that customer-perceived quality is one of the four variables that has by far the greatest importance to profitability measured as return on invested capital. Figure 17 shows how profitability varies with changes in customer-perceived quality.

Within the framework of PIMS, quality is measured in terms of both product-related and service-related variables. Each variable is assigned a points score which expresses its importance to the customer's perception of quality. A comparison is then made with the three largest competitors, to whom corresponding scores are assigned, and an expression for relative product quality is derived from this. The word relative in this context refers to how the quality of a company's products stands in relation to its chief competitors'.

Suppliers' evaluations of quality always tend to overrate the importance of product-related variables, in other words the performance of the product itself. Customers, on the other hand, put more emphasis on service-related variables than do people in the supplier's organization. This means that all organizations have a built-in tendency to misjudge the importance of customer-perceived quality variables, to overrate the importance of the product and underrate that of service.

The term quality has suffered to some extent from over-use. The fact is that high quality is not always the same thing as ingenious design and high performance. The customer relates value to a price, and that is why it is important to be able to segment a market, to divide it into sub-sets of customers whose value judgements are similar. The quality-price relationship is not the same for the package tourist as for the business traveller.

A man with a family and a low income uses a different set of values when choosing a car than a high-salaried bachelor. Nevertheless, interest in quality has undoubtedly focused the attention of companies on the importance of customer-perceived value.

Quality circles emerged at the beginning of the 1980s as the new faith that Japanese companies had embraced to compete successfully with Americans and Europeans.

A quality circle usually consists of 10 to 12 employees who work as a team and have a common goal for their activities. The task of a quality circle is to identify the need structures of the users of its services, and gradually improve what it delivers. The members of a quality circle meet for a few hours every week to try to identify problems and work systematically to solve them and improve their performance.

The phenomenon of quality circles must be viewed against its historical background. During the period of reconstruction in the late 1940s and the 1950s, Japan produced goods that were regarded as copies and of poor quality. This offended Japanese national pride and prompted an all-out effort in the area of quality development. Thus from being stigmatized as cheap and nasty just a few decades ago, Japanese goods have now surged to a position of being synonymous with high quality.

Quality is one of the most widely used buzz-words in modern management. The term has become a management fad, and therefore needs to be carefully defined in relation to the context in which it is used.

The word quality is often used to express a general desire for greater efficiency. In other cases it may mean more efficient production or better penetration of the market. But within the broad area of meaning of the word quality we can distinguish two principal senses in which it can appropriately be used.

The first is production-related quality: zero defects, 'lean' production, etc. The second is customer-perceived quality, which is what influences the frequency of repeat purchases, etc. Figure 18 illustrates how these two senses of the word quality affect a company's profit-and-loss account.

Research has clearly shown that quality pays: the extra revenue earned by offering better quality than your competitors, whether in product-related or service-related variables, is greater than the extra cost incurred in achieving it. This is a known fact.

Figure 18 'Quality' as perceived by the customer and as related to production.

Finally, I would like to emphasize another known fact, the fact that organizations tend to overrate the importance of product-related quality at the expense of service-related quality. Figure 19, which comes from PIMS research, agrees well with the author's own experience. It shows how suppliers of a product attach more importance to product-related variables than do the buyers of the product.

We can conclude with a checklist of suitable steps in a process of quality improvement:

1 Establish who the customers are.
2 Define customers' utility functions (demands).
3 Define products and services supplied by your organization.
4 Look for opportunities for improvement, gaps between current product and utility functions.
5 Solve problems in sequence.
6 Modify operating procedures.
7 Deliver better products or services.
8 Measure customer reactions to verify improvement.
9 Time marches on. Go back to step one and start over.

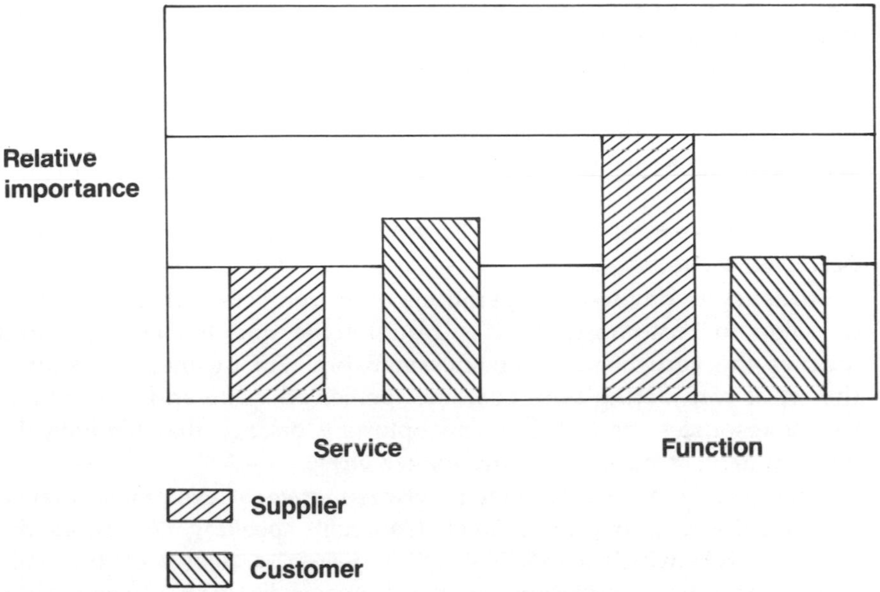

Relative
importance

Service   Function

▨ Supplier

▨ Customer

Figure 19 Suppliers underrate service compared to product. People in the supplier's own organization attach less importance than their customers to service-related variables, and more importance to functional product variables.

RATIONALIZATION

By rationalization we mean the measures to achieve either the same production with less consumption of resources or increased production with the same consumption of resources. By resources we mean capital and costs.

Strategic development was at one time strongly associated with cost rationalization through economies of scale. Thinking on the subject of high market shares was based on the need to produce large quantities in order to reduce the cost per unit. Rationalization of the cost mass is a necessary everyday phenomenon, which occasionally requires an extra effort to prevent a company's profitability from suffering on that account.

The true meaning of economy is management of scarce resources. The term economy thus implies a continuous demand for rationalization, that is orientation towards shrinking resources.

The difference between economy and business is that economy is concerned solely with utilization of resources, whereas business also includes the creation of value for customers, as well as the dynamics of the organization. The pendulum principle makes it easy to swing too far to one extreme or the other, for example by underestimating the value of rationalization to long-term profitability. Rationalization is apt to get forgotten in periods of rapid development.

The term operational efficiency refers to the management of resources in current business. It is actually a synonym for continuous rationalization, expressing how efficiently you make use of the structure of investments or whatever that you have to work with. The problem that is apt to arise in trying to achieve operational efficiency is that it is easy to neglect your company's strategic aims and customer-perceived value.

Efficiency in day-to-day operations often conflicts with the criterion of value to customers. This is troublesome and a challenge, and touches the very heart of businessmanship. For businessmanship is the art of considering both customer-perceived value and the rational use of resources, and striking an optimum balance that benefits the development of business in the longer term.

Some people make a distinction between strategic level, tactical level, and functional or operative level. Generally speaking we ignore the tactical level, which lacks instructive value; it does not normally involve any major problems. It may however be useful to make the following distinction in this context:

Operative efficiency requires the ability to do things right with minimum input of resources, for example to move a person from Manhattan to Kennedy Airport (whether he actually wants to go there or not); while functional strategy requires the ability to do the right things by relating the function concerned to overall goals and strategies. According to this reasoning, every function (department) must relate its goals to the strategies of the organization as a whole and develop patterns of action that support the aims of the business.

To simplify somewhat, we can say that operative control is control of the activities of an organization within given terms of reference, while strategic control, on the other hand, has to do with stating the terms of reference.

RELATIVE COST POSITION

This term is often abbreviated to RCP. It states the costs of a business unit or function in relation to those of its competitors. RCP is usually expressed as an index obtained by dividing the costs of a given business unit by the average costs of each of its competitors. An index of 1.0 thus means that the costs of a business unit exactly match those of its competitors. An index of less than 1.0 indicates a cost advantage, while a figure above 1.0 means a cost disadvantage.

RCP can be analysed for a single product, for a product line, for a business unit, for a company as a whole or for some function within a company, for example, the in-flight service in an airline company or the marketing in a manufacturing company. The costs included in the analysis may comprise variable costs, total costs, or some combination of elements in the cost structure of the business.

RCP analysis is one of the two corner-stones of competition analysis. The other is analysis of customer-perceived value. As has been emphasized in many other sections of this glossary, businessmanship is a combination of creative generation of value, and persistent, painstaking resource management. Similarly, the two corner-stones of analysis deal with customer-perceived value and costs compared to those of one or more competitors.

A large, international, mechanical engineering corporation recently ran a study of customer-perceived value. It revealed that the corporation was inferior to its chief competitor on the after-sales service side, that is in spare part prices, spare part delivery times, and price and promptness of technical service.

Concurrently with the development of strategies to improve the after-sales situation, the company has now mounted a study of its relative cost position. What this study relates to is the one competitor that the corporation meets on all its major markets.

The results of an RCP analysis may for example show:

1 That production costs expressed in hourly wage rates are higher than a competitor's because you are producing in a high-cost environment (the Netherlands, for example) while your competitor does most of his manufacturing in a low-cost environment (for example, Greece). Production costs in the form of labour and capital costs account for about one-third of sales value. The wage cost disadvantage, calculated on this basis, is about 4 per cent compared to your main competitor.

2 Components are bought from all over the world, and a thorough analysis shows that there is no significant difference in this area. The index for this factor is thus 1.0.

3 You manage your central administrative costs much more efficiently than your competitor does. Your own company is of Scandinavian origin, which in this case means it has a slimmed down central administrative apparatus with few staff and effective computerized systems for both accounting and logistics. The analysis shows that administrative efficiency gives you a relative cost advantage of 1.5 per cent of total sales value.

4 Analysis of marketing costs points to definite inefficiencies in your own company. You have established a large number of sales companies all over the world, which have grown somewhat bureaucratic. The productivity of your head office marketing organization and sales companies is low compared to your competitor's, and the figures reveal a relative cost disadvantage of as much as 5 per cent of sales value.

The foregoing simple example shows how an RCP analysis can be built up. The difficult part is not the theory behind the analysis, but getting hold of competitors' cost figures. This is often easier in a business like civil aviation or consultancy. In the airline business, for example, you may choose to compare your position with that of a company with which you have little direct competition.

RESOURCES: COSTS AND CAPITAL

The heading summarizes the two main kinds of resources we usually speak of, namely costs and capital. For a better understanding of what they mean, however, we need to break them down into their components. Capital is composed of:

- bills receivable from customers
- fixed assets
- inventory

while the cost mass can similarly be broken down into some main cost categories:

- personnel costs
- capital costs
- material costs
- overhead

Rational use of resources is one of the two chief areas of businessmanship. The other is creation of value (*see also* VALUE).

Management of resources used to be the main objective of strategy. Advantages of scale and economies through mass production were the key concepts during the long period when demand generally exceeded supply. But much less attention was paid to capital than to costs, the reason being that capital costs were small on account of low interest rates. That aspect of the situation, together with many others, changed in the mid-1970s, and a lot has been learned about the use of capital since then. The relationship is most simply expressed by the return-on-investment formula:

$$\text{ROI} = \frac{\text{Revenues} - \text{Costs}}{\text{Capital}}$$

The term revenues here represents the creation of value for the customer, while costs and capital stand for use of resources. A holistic view of business involves the ability to strike the right balance between these three basic elements of business management.

There is a close correlation between the terms capital and investment. The latter word is also used in the sense of tied-up or committed capital. Capital is shown on the asset side of the balance sheet under the headings of fixed assets (production equipment, buildings or whatever), inventory (raw materials, work in progress and stocks of finished goods) and bills receivable, which are administered by techniques known collectively as cash management.

Resource control (see below) thus calls for a whole range of special skills, especially in the area of production.

One resource that does not appear on the balance sheet is non-financial capital in the form of know-how. This has grown much more important because non-financial capital is the principal asset of many companies today, and its management calls for very special skills.

Resource control

Synonyms of resource control are decision-making, resource allocation, functional strategies and policies.

The term resource control is not so widely used today because it echoes the control mentality that prevailed in an earlier, more technocratic epoch of business management. The very word control carries associations of centralized direction, and was indeed one of the favourite expressions of the classic bureaucratic school.

Coupled with the word resources, however, control has come to mean primarily the utilization of resources to guide business as effectively as possible in the direction one wants it to go. By resources, we mean costs and capital; to be more specific, the term resource or business control involves detail decisions on use of resources, for example:

- pricing
- volume of production
- investment in development
- new products
- computer systems
- personnel
- bills receivable
- bills payable
- capital tied up in fixed assets
- capital tied up in inventory

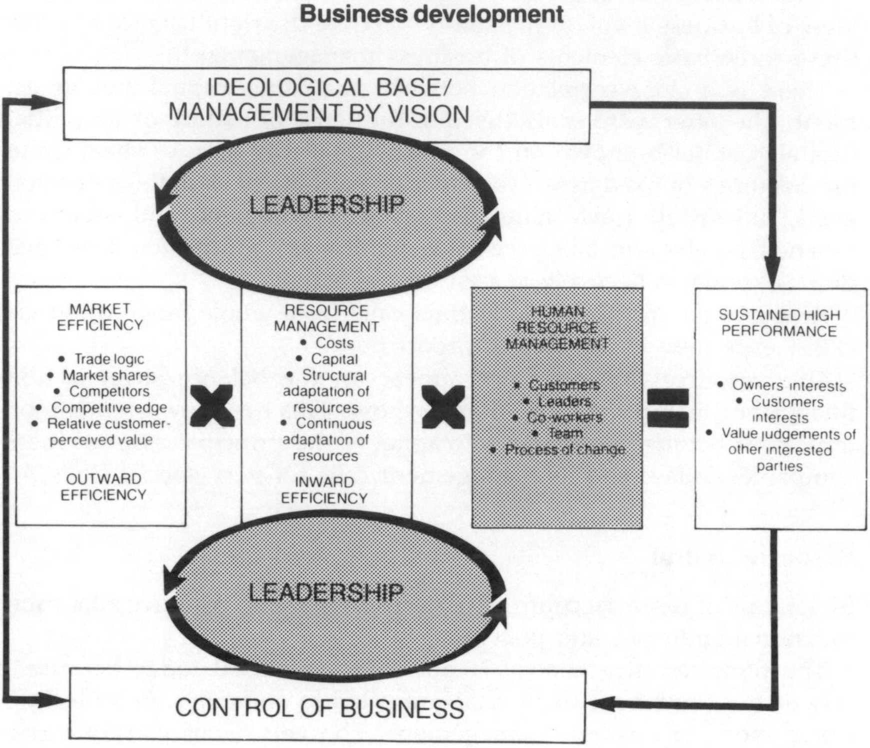

Business development

Figure 20 Business development.

Source: B. Karlöf and S. Söderberg, *The Challenge of Leadership*.

- communications
- marketing
- investments
- organization
- advertising

The list of examples makes no claim to be complete, and some of the items overlap. The important thing to remember is that resource control means a body of detail decisions, all of which support a defined corporate mission and overall strategy.

SCENARIO

A scenario is defined as an assumed or possible course of events in a given area. The scenario form is used as an alternative to forecasts of an extrapolatory nature. Forecasts are predictions of the future based on known trends and known facts. The forecast method, however, is incapable of predicting discontinuities and is not conducive to the free thinking that is essential at times when there is a need to delay instead of plan.

Forecasting was refined and played an important part in the age of technocratic planning (a technocrat is one who applies rational technical or economic criteria without regard to human values). During the period from World War II up to the mid-1970s when the future was predictable, forecasting methods of all kinds seemed to work admirably as a tool for strategy determination. As part of the radical reappraisal that had to be made after the crises of the 1970s, traditional forecasting methods were also critically reviewed. What struck heads of businesses most forcefully in those days was the tendency of forecasts to prolong existing trends, which pointed to investment in increased capacity and other forms of expansion.

Such investments showed a very poor return when the demand curve flattened out, leading to overcapacity in many industries. A need was then felt for other ways of assessing the future. The scenario form had proved effective for this purpose in two respects:

1 In the first place, it is possible to state a probable line of development on the basis of predictions and assumptions.
2 In the second place, it is possible to visualize alternative courses of events, and use them as the basis for intelligent discussion.

The scenario, then, is a description of a future set of circumstances. It may refer to business or some other form of activity, and is based on a selection of assumptions and forecasts about future events.

In the field of strategy the scenario form is generally used to predict possible structural changes in an industry and probable competitive situations. Here the scenario generally serves as a platform for creative discussions, strategic thinking and, of course, strategy determination.

The forecasts and assumptions on which a scenario is constructed must embrace all the factors that have a bearing on the future of a business. One of the most important advantages of the scenario is that both extremes and probable developments can be taken into account in an intelligent discussion based on the assumptions and forecasts underlying the scenario.

We usually speak in terms of pessimistic, probable and optimistic scenarios. The probable scenario is the one on which decisions and strategy formulations are usually based, whereas the extreme cases help management to identify the factors that are relevant to the future of the business.

What follows here is an example of a scenario for a car manufacturer.

The purpose of this scenario was to try to identify issues of importance to the development department of the manufacturer concerned.

Assumptions about broad developments

Economic situation
- at the end of or on the way out of a recession
- purchasing power much the same as now
- smaller income differentials
- no dramatic changes in oil prices
- new newly industrialized countries emerging

Political situation
- peace, stability
- Eastern Europe awakening
- market economy stronger

Social situation
- greater equality between the sexes
- higher level of education
- healthy lifestyle
- renaissance of the family
- crowded conditions

Environment
- pollution
- environmental damage
- strong awareness

Scenario 1993–1998

1 No new energy crisis, but possibly higher energy prices.
2 Greater environmental awareness, leading to decisions on environmental issues.
3 Hitherto underdeveloped countries developing their own car industries and generating a constant pressure on the down-market segment.
4 Japanese moving towards the up-market segment. New types of cars, like minivans, appearing.
5 Role of importers diminished, tending to concentrate on marketing and marketing support.
6 Sociological and political factors point to need for stronger profile in the areas of environment, customer care and quality.
7 Congestion in big cities critical; this will affect the behaviour of commuters who do not need to use cars for on-the-job transportation.
8 The media will be concentrated and internationalized, and advertising messages will therefore grow more uniform. The importance of the TV medium will grow, especially in view of the congruence between choice of channel and profile.
9 Good economic growth, accompanied by somewhat heightened awareness

of resource conservation, will favour economical cars compared to the late 1980s.

10 Political factors will encourage stable demand and open up good opportunities for business in Eastern Europe.

11 Non-polluting vehicles will be preferred. Non-pulluting and ergonomic manufacturing facilities will be advantageous image-wise.

12 Sociologically, greater sexual equality and the preferences of the 1950s and 1960s generations will favour sensible cars with less fancy trimmings.

SEGMENTATION AND DIFFERENTIATION

These two terms can suitably be defined as follows:

1 Segmentation means division of a total market into sub-sets characterized by similarity of demand.

2 Differentiation means a special formulation of a product (goods and/or services) and price to match the demand and cost structure respectively of the segment for which they are intended.

Segmentation and differentiation are linked terms, one having to do with demand and the other with supply.

A segment, then, is a subgroup characterized by shared evaluation of the utility functions of a product or service. The segmentation process can be initiated in two phases:

1 Grouping of individuals with the same evaluations of utility functions.

2 Labelling or identifying the segments.

Companies often begin by labelling, which sometimes leads to erroneous segmentation.

Segmentation has proved to be a much more intricate process than marketers originally thought. Traditional methods of market analysis do not give automatic answers to the problems of segmentation, for a segment is not the same thing as a statistical group, although it may be practical to work with such groups. We speak for example of large companies that need a particular kind of service, medium-sized companies that need another kind, and small companies that need a third kind.

The segmentation process can be viewed in two ways. Either you separate a homogeneous market comprising a large number of individuals into segments, or else you group a large number of individuals into a smaller number of operative segments. This is illustrated in the phases shown in Figure 21.

Such a breakdown by size is only an approximation, or rough estimate, of something else that we are really looking for. The thing we

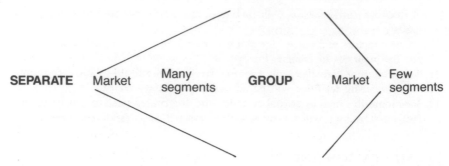

Figure 21 A homogeneous market can be separated into a number of segments, and a market with many small segments can be grouped into a smaller number of operational segments.

are trying to identify in terms of size of company may for example be the level of knowledge of the management or degree of willingness to buy a particular service. Such differences in demand usually have nothing to do with the statistical groupings as such, but are often assumed to match those groupings reasonably well, or at any rate well enough for marketing purposes.

Another way to explain the use of statistical groupings is that willingness to buy simply cannot be ascertained without comprehensive polling, so estimates are used instead.

Marketing aimed at private consumers often uses other statistical criteria such as age group, religion, sex, or place of residence. These, too, are approximations of actual market segments; the statistical groupings are assumed to correspond to types of buying behaviour. Intelligent segmentation requires a greater measure of creative ability, a fact which is often neglected.

SAS's identification of the special needs of business travellers is an example of segmentation and consequent differentiation. The same thing was done a few years earlier by an American domestic airline, which managed to satisfy the demand of private persons for low-price air travel by utilizing the great increase in carrying capacity that its new fleet of aircraft had given it in combination with off-peak flights that were little used by business travellers.

The resegmentation undertaken by speciality car makers offers a splendid example of how different segments of a market can be identified and the product differentiated accordingly:

- Audi moved from the position of being a manufacturer of fairly ordinary family cars to another, more up-market, segment of family cars that were more comfortable to ride in and more fun to drive, thus encroaching on the traditional bailiwick of Mercedes-Benz.
- Saab took a slightly different approach; with the launch of the 9000

model, it went in for a sportier type of family car in the part of the market traditionally dominated by BMW.

By these exercises in differentiation, both companies have succeeded in attracting a clientele with higher purchasing power, and have been able to raise their prices and improve their margins.

Most people have a tendency to associate differentiation with upgrading, that is a change in a product to bring it to a more advanced and expensive level. Segmentation, however, does not necessarily mean upgrading, but simply a concentration on some specific group with a homogeneous need structure.

Examples of differentiation that have led to simplification of the product are a domestic airline's drive to attract private passengers, and the establishment of the People's Express airline in the United States. Both companies identified groups looking for a lower-priced product with a lower level of service. We find the same kind of thing in the insurance world, where some insurance policies have grown so comprehensive that they now include kinds of coverage that not all customers require.

A creative attempt to divide an existing target group into homogeneous areas of demand usually bears fruit. This is often done in markets for fast-moving consumer goods, but perhaps not often enough in other industries. On the other hand, segmentation and differentiation can be overdone, as you will find if you try to choose between all the different kinds of babies' nappies or sun-tan lotions on offer.

SERVICE COMPANIES AND SOFTWARE COMPANIES

Production of services has grown in importance as the proportions of gross national product (the total value of a country's production) accounted for by agricultural and industrial production have declined. Theories have therefore been formulated about companies that sell services, software and know-how.

The term service company focuses interest on the value of what is delivered. Services are often seen as the opposite of products. Services may be unskilled and industrialized, or highly skilled and personalized.

The term service company in itself gives no clue to the know-how content of the services delivered. Some services, like computerized banking and air travel, involve heavy capital investment. Others, like medical care, legal advice and management consultancy, require little or no capital but an extremely high level of knowledge on the part of those who supply the services.

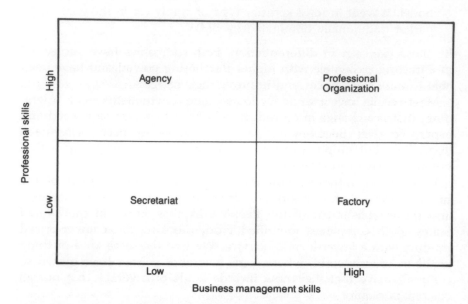

Figure 22 Software companies fall into four main types. The agency is a congenial workplace for professional people, but has low survival potential. The secretariat rates low on both professional and managerial skills. The factory does not have to depend on the problem-solving abilities of individuals. The professional organization is an ideal environment for the development of new skilled employees.

The service component of industrial products is growing proportionately larger in almost all industries. This can include equipment maintenance, after-sales service, financing and other services associated with the actual delivery of hardware.

It is for these reasons that the term software company has recently come into currency. It is used to distinguish mass production of standard products with low information content from one-off production of goods or services with a high information content.

The specific problem of software companies is the difficulty of combining professional skills with management ability. In extreme cases the professional skill is synonymous with the corporate mission. High-tech software companies have chronic difficulty in recruiting people willing and able to assume the role of chief executive.

The term software company should be used with some care, because many industrial products today have a high software content. There are no obvious generalizations that can be made from different high-tech industries, so other and more distinctive terms will undoubtedly be coined in the future.

'Knowledge is power', as Francis Bacon wrote.

STRATEGIC MANAGEMENT

Strategic management ability involves a combination of five things:

Ability to see patterns in what is happening. The terms holistic vision and 'helicopterability' often refer to the ability to recognize the interplay between customer needs, customer demand, competitors and their products, and one's own company and its ability to satisfy customers' needs. By this definition, analysis is obviously a part of strategic thinking.

But the complexity and breadth of variation of the analysis make it difficult to reduce to models. The greater the business strategist's ability to abstract, the more clearly the relationships in the business pattern emerge. The ability to go from concretion to abstraction and back again is thus an important aspect of strategic competence. By using this ability, the strategist can grasp patterns in the environment that can be used to trace the need for change in his own company.

Ability to identify need for change. Changes in companies nowadays take place in many more dimensions than used to be the case. For most companies, change was formerly to all intents and purposes synonymous with expansion. Changes are composed of a many-faceted set of variables ranging from cost-effectiveness in production to differentiation of the product range; they also involve many 'soft' variables, like quality and attitudes to risk-taking.

Identification of a need for change calls for two abilities:

1 Being alert to trends arising out of known factors in the industry in question.
2 Using intelligence and creativity to combine known and unknown variables and thereby to achieve a state of readiness for unforeseen contingencies and to recognize opportunities to improve the company's ability to compete.

The easy but inadequate solution, of course, is to predict that the situation tomorrow will be the same as it is today. We all have an innate tendency to take 'just like now only more so' as our model for assessing the future.

Ability to devise strategies for change. Strategy determination, or strategy formulation as it is sometimes called, is both an intellectual process, a process of winning acceptance, and a creative process. Most of this book deals with the art of strategy.

Ability to use tools for change. Knowledge of the components of strategic management and some knowledge of traditional attitudes to questions of strategy are excellent aids to good management. Most strategy models are constructed on a foundation of operations research which, to the new way of thinking, makes them suspect. But, if nothing else, a good all-round education in strategies should include a knowledge of both the old and new BCG (Boston Consulting Group) MATRICES, MCKINSEY'S 7S MODEL and the EXPERIENCE CURVE (*see* Models section for details). Some models of this type still have an impressive explanatory value, especially in certain areas of strategy analysis.

Ability to implement strategies. All the mental effort and creativity you put into devising a strategy will be so much waste of time unless you can put your ideas into effect. This apparently obvious statement has not in fact been obvious for so very long, which explains the over-emphasis sometimes given to strategy implementation in recent years. Conversely, action unsupported by structure of thought is usually fairly pointless. Running at high speed without first deciding which way to run is generally just as ineffectual as high-powered thinking that is not followed by action.

Structure and dynamism, in other words, are the two essentials that must be paired to bring any proposed change to a successful conclusion.

With the definition of strategic management that I have adopted, a major problem becomes evident right from the start. Traditional Western business philosophy leans heavily towards maximizing short-term profits and eliminating risks. A most difficult problem connected with the chosen definition, as with all work in strategy, is that of finding ways to measure the effects of strategic management ability and to set rewards commensurate with the resulting changes. This applies especially to operations in investment-intensive industries where turnaround times are long and it takes quite a while for the effects to show up.

'By their fruits ye shall know them.' In most organizations, the fruits are operative results. Most executives are promoted up the organizational ladder on the basis of their operational achievements, so it is not hard to understand why current criteria of business success are so heavily influenced by career patterns and the demand for results.

One great problem is that executives in general do not receive training in strategic management and therefore do not develop their strategic thinking to keep pace with their advancement in the corporate hierarchy. There is a great deal to be said for revising the criteria of success as executives climb higher up the career ladder. They need to have their strategic thinking ability exercised by being given opportunities to study different strategic situations. An average chief executive may only be faced with two or three strategic situations in his whole career.

It is an often overlooked fact that strategic management ability depends in no small degree on this very kind of strategic experience. Creating or simulating opportunities for strategic thinking is thus an important factor in leadership development.

STRATEGY

The term strategy is derived from the art of war, where it means the planning and execution of national or power bloc policies by the use of all available resources. By analogy, the term is used in the general sense of taking a broad, long-term approach. The word has been adopted into the terminology of business management, where it has gradually acquired the meaning of what was formerly called policy or business policy.

Strategy, then, is a choice of markets, products, investment structures, etc. aiming at long-term profitability. Operative management, on the other hand, is action aiming at short-term profitability.

Resource management was long the standard concept of strategy. Its origins can be traced back to an insight gained by the commanding officer of the US Army Air Force's Wright Patterson Base in Dayton, Ohio, back in 1926. He discovered that unit costs fell by about 20 per cent every time he doubled the production of anything. This discovery led to the formulation of the EXPERIENCE CURVE (see Models), which in turn spawned a number of models based on long production runs and low unit costs. One of these is the BCG MATRIX. The idea behind that model, like so many others, was that a high market share makes it possible to rationalize production on the basis of long runs, thereby achieving low unit costs which in turn lead to high competitive ability and profitability.

These conclusions were naturally correct with reference to the situation that prevailed up to the mid-1970s, when the pressure of competition was low compared to what it is today. The chief problems of organized activity during and after World War II had to do with administering vast quantities of people, capital and materials. Logistic systems were refined, and techniques of operations analysis were successfully applied to these problems of optimization, that is of finding the most efficient way to do something or dispose of something.

After World War II there were worldwide shortages of goods, and demand could be taken for granted. In that situation resource management was the principal problem, and strategy appeared to consist of a choice between alternative ways to grow.

Portfolio strategy therefore came to dominate corporate strategic thinking. In many diversified corporations, in those with business units established in different industries, the problems that exercised top management were concerned with deciding which business units to invest in. The competitive element within the framework of an individual business unit was of minor importance in the prevailing situation of excess demand.

Portfolio strategy

Briefly, portfolio strategy is concerned with:

- acquisitions in new industries
- reinforcement of existing business units by acquisition
- phasing out involvement in unwanted industries
- selling business units that can find more favourable structures elsewhere
- allocating resources in the form of capital and costs
- ensuring that business units are strategically managed
- taking advantage of synergy effects between business units in the portfolio

The need to be able to compete effectively has gradually become more apparent, and the emphasis of strategy has therefore shifted from portfolio to business unit level. The issues there are of an entirely different nature, the object of strategy being to create competitive advantages that will enable the business unit to reach set goals.

Business strategy

The purpose of strategy is to achieve a lasting competitive edge that will give good profitability. Strategy consists of an integrated pattern of actions designed to reach set goals by co-ordinating and channelling a company's resources. The term strategy development refers to this whole process, which comprises:

1 Definition of corporate mission.
2 Concretization of visions in terms of goals.
3 Formulation and implementation of strategies for reaching those goals.

One of the great arts of strategy is that of translating strategic thinking into concrete action and achieving high efficiency in the implementation phase.

FUNCTIONAL STRATEGIES are used to marshall the resources of the functions or departments of which a company consists. It is important to break down portfolio strategies into business strategies and thence to functional strategies, because the actual input of resources usually occurs at the functional level. The basic functions of business management are development, production, marketing and administration. These in turn may be subdivided into such specialist departments as information, personnel or data processing. The term operative efficiency, as distinct from functional strategy, is applied to short-term action to 'tune' the organization.

Discussions of strategy are often confused by thè fact that means at a higher level become ends at a lower level, and so on. This can be called the hierarchy of strategy; it means for example that if goals are set and strategies for reaching those goals are devised at portfolio level, those strategies in their turn become the goals of the business units in the portfolio, which then devise their own strategies for reaching them. The resulting business strategies are then translated into goals for each of the business unit's component functions.

In present-day development processes, general strategy development is usually followed by a phase of organization development designed to improve the state of the organization in such a way that it will be better fitted to compete and develop its business.

There has been a marked tendency for the profession of strategy as it is practised to deviate from businessmanship. In my view this is an unfortunate tendency, because strategy ought to be the same thing as businessmanship, with a field of view that is wider and longer than in other forms of businessmanship.

STRATEGY ANALYSIS

Managers and executives often seek a structure for an analysis of their business that will provide the overview they need. Management consultants have developed structures that can be used to satisfy this need. For example:

1 Portfolio
2 Trade logic
3 Business unit

The term business unit can be analysed in its turn into four parts: ideological base, outward efficiency, inward efficiency and strategic management, all of which can be further segmented.

1 Ideological base
  (a) Vision
  (b) Goals

(c) Corporate mission and strategy
(d) Customer-perceived quality

2 Outward efficiency (markets)
   (a) Needs
   (b) Market share
   (c) New business
   (d) Customer-perceived quality

3 Inward efficiency (resources)
   (a) Costs
   (b) Capital
   (c) Productivity

4 Strategic management
   (a) Ability to chart a course
   (b) Ability to organize with reference to the chosen course
   (c) Ability to motivate people in the organization and arouse their enthusiasm

These are the things that the chief executive of a company ought to know in order to have a grasp of his business. A company is a legal entity and usually represents some kind of portfolio, that is a collection of business units. A portfolio is not in an industry but each of its business units is. The analysis should therefore begin with a description of the portfolio. A portfolio comprises a number of business units whose main analytical variables are:

1 The attractiveness of the industry in terms of profitability and development
2 The position of the business unit in its industry.

The term TRADE LOGIC is defined on page 141. An understanding of trade logic is all too often neglected; a consideration of the relevant trade logic can enhance your thinking and give you a clearer view of your own business.

The business unit itself, of course, is the main issue. To get a better grasp of it, you can divide the analysis into considerations of ideological base, outward efficiency, inward efficiency and strategic management.

The *ideological base* is the vision (dream or future memory) towards which the leader wants to guide his business. He does so with the help of goals (milestones on the road to the vision) which are expressed in terms of money, market shares and customer-perceived quality. The route is determined by strategy, while the corporate mission – the expression of business philosophy – is defined by needs, customers, product and competitive edge.

Outward efficiency consists in the knowledge of customers' need structures and how well the company is satisfying them. Market share and trends therein are one way to measure this. Outward efficiency also includes the creation of new business. Ability to do so gives an indication of how businesslike and expansive the company is.

Inward efficiency means the cost position of the business unit, in other words, how it is using its capital and how its total productivity is developing. All these criteria can to some extent be related to the performance of competitors.

Finally, *strategic management* ability is a relatively new analytical variable which has to do with diagnosis of the management's strategic ability. This refers not only to the situation at the time of diagnosis, but also to possibilities for development. Management must have the ability to choose the right course and steer the whole organization along it.

This approach to achieving a businesslike synthesis has proved effective in practice. The analysis can be refined, and its scope must of course be adapted to the situation in hand. The important thing is to be able to grasp the whole picture without getting bogged down in details.

SYNERGY

The word synergy is derived from synergism, which in biological science means co-operation between different organs. Synergy means the strategic advantages that are gained when two or more business units are combined in the portfolio of a group of companies. Operations become more efficient in the sense that they generate more value or cost less. The combined effect is more advantageous than the sum of the individual strategies.

Many people involved in management dislike the term synergy. There are several near-synonyms which are used with slightly different shades of meaning:

- strategic lever
- interrelations
- cost advantages
- rationalization gains

The term synergy was popularized by Igor Ansoff and used as a rationale to explain the structure of groups of companies. The 1950s and 1960s saw the rise of many conglomerates, i.e. portfolios of disparate business units. At that time the thinking was done and the decisions made at group management level. As a result, group managements tended to be fairly large and to include a number of staff departments. The savings as a result of 'shared costs' were thus considerable, and it was thus easy to point to synergies in the group management functions. Corporations, moreover, often felt a need to justify their global expansion. When they acquired a company, they felt they simply had to explain to that company and the world at large why they had acquired it.

In fact the world is full of alleged synergies cited as justification for acquisitions. Growth by acquisition is often felt to be stimulating and tempting, and is certainly beneficial to a market economy. Acquisition as a method of growth, as distinct from organic growth, is a kind of businessmanship practised by people with a flair for structural solutions. Through acquisitions and divestments they release values that the stock market might otherwise have overlooked. This is sometimes called corporate raiding; it is regarded by many as a ruthless exploitation of people and of business structures that somebody else has built up. There may be a great temptation to cite synergies of various kinds as motives for buying a company. In fact this happens so often that the term synergy has fallen into disrepute, which is why people prefer to use other expressions.

A *synergistic portfolio* is a group of business units under common ownership which are strategically related to each other. Its opposite is a *diversified portfolio* or conglomerate. One example of a synergistic portfolio is an airline which also owns hotels and operates ground transport and airport services. Another is a consultant firm which offers management, computer system and marketing consultancy services.

Synergies can be found in various functions with regard to both costs and added value for customers. Examples of such functions are R&D, production, sales, advertising and administration. In a recent merger between two stockbroking firms, the smaller one had been about to invest heavily in computer systems, while the larger had just done so. In this case they achieved synergy by sharing the new resource.

Another kind of synergy is seen when a large airline acquires a hotel chain in order to be able to offer complete 'travel packages' to its passengers. The added value from the traveller's point of view is greater than the sum of what the airline and the hotel chain would have offered separately.

Finally, the reader should beware of placing exaggerated faith in synergetic effects. Compromises, lack of flexibility and delays often eat up the calculated cost advantages. Economies of scale often obey Gresham's Law: quantitative analysis always drives out qualitative analysis. This means that economies of scale which do not take creation of customer value into account are easy to quantify, but perception of value is not.

TRADE LOGIC

Trade logic, sometimes referred to as the business logic of an industry, is invaluable in helping the business strategist to understand the key factors for success in a given industry.

Briefly summarized, the purpose of trade logic is to understand the key factors that lead to sustained profitability in a given industry. An understanding of trade logic gives you a good strategy development process and more effective strategy analysis.

Trade logic is defined below in the form of five questions. There is no generally received definition, so the meaning of the term may vary according to need.

1 What is the nature of the need structure that generates demand?
2 What factors in the product contribute to success and to what extent do they include product mystique, that is non-rational factors?
3 How is the industry structured?
4 What entry and exit barriers exist?
5 What are the key factors for success in the industry?

Structure in question 3 refers to the technological and economic factors that determine the kind and degree of competition in the industry. It is the result of dynamic interaction between various actors in the industry, namely:

• suppliers
• buyers
• competitors
• substitute products
• influence of national and local government
• establishment of new companies
• disappearance of existing companies

Variations between industries can be analysed in the above terms for purposes of risk and potential profit assessment.

Sometimes it is useful to assess the social importance of an industry. Steam engine manufacturing, for example, was important 100 years ago and railways 50 years ago. The data consultancy industry has already seen its best days, whereas the electronics industry is still growing.

An understanding of trade logic is of fundamental importance to the business strategist. His chances of operating successfully in an industry are enormously improved if he possesses that knowledge.

Conversely, it must be noted that quick promotion in companies often leads to the appointment of managers who do not know enough about the trade logic of an industry to be able to do their jobs effectively.

Newly appointed managers often have to learn the industry-specific success factors the hard way. Some industries have extremely complicated patterns of logic that cannot be understood without analysis in depth, and it is one of the management consultant's most difficult tasks to learn the trade logic of his client's industry.

TRADE MARK

A trade mark is a word, mark, symbol or design that identifies a product or differentiates a company and its product from others.

The importance of trade marks has long been underrated, especially in manufacturing industry. Trade marks like BMW, ICI and IBM have great value in themselves because they influence potential customers' perceptions of the reality that those companies' products represent. A trade mark is thus charged with image (the outside world's perception of reality).

The function of a trade mark is to contribute to marketing (creation of demand). By establishing a strong trade mark, a company can generate demand without having to struggle hard for it by expensive marketing.

Another way of putting it is that customers' expectations of quality are built into the trade mark. This can produce two effects:

1 Customers ask for goods or services because their expectations have been aroused by hearsay or first-hand experience.
2 If the expectations aroused by a trade mark are much higher than the reality of the product, this can easily lead to disappointment.

Trade marks were neglected during the technocratic, rational epoch of management. Their importance to marketing was not properly understood. The savings banks, for example, neglected a trade mark that at one time was strongly associated with the idea of regular saving from birth. In fact, the savings banks have now lost their position, once taken for granted, as the place where private citizens kept their money from womb to tomb. In recent times there has been a resurgence of insight into the importance of trade marks, which have now become a stock weapon in the arsenal of business strategy.

Trade marks have two effects related to business:

1 They create demand and are thus an invaluable aid to marketing.
2 Their aura arouses expectations which must be satisfied.

The idea of image (outsiders' perception of reality) has a strong effect

Figure 23 Examples of trade marks.

on reactions to trade marks. When people hear a name like Fiat, Mercedes, SAS or Aeroflot, it conjures up associations that influence their expectations to a high degree. The establishment and maintenance of a trade mark are therefore an important part of business management. This can be done, for example, by polling customers and working actively on quality.

If you are responsible for a function within a large organization, you might care to reflect on the question of what associations the name of your department conjures up in the minds of other members of the organization.

VALUE

One of the old-fashioned terms that were given a new lease of life by the hardening climate of competition in the late 1970s was customer-perceived value. Other terms are used for the same thing, but it is the very foundation of the idea of business development.

Whatever you sell or offer to a market – whether you are a politician, a businessman, a trade union boss or a leader of a religious revival – you are offering the person to whom you address your message (let us call him/her your customer) a product or service of value to them. To get this value, customers must make a sacrifice (pay a price).

The vertical axis of the graph in Figure 24 represents the value offered, and the horizontal axis represents the price paid. Within the shaded diagonal band, the customer feels she is getting value for money. Customers at the lower left end of the band get relatively little value, but also pay a relatively small price. Here we find the customer who buys one of the cheap small cars mass produced by Ford, Renault, Fiat or Volkswagen.

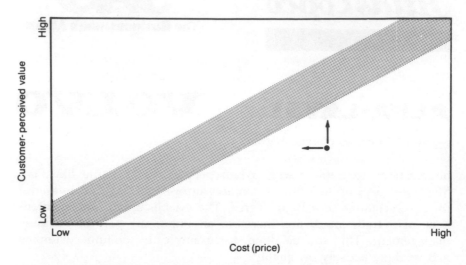

Figure 24 Relationship between price and value. The value graph shows the relationship between the price of a product and the value the customer places on it. In the shaded band the customer feels he is getting value for his money.

The customer at the top right end of the band gets a lot of value, but pays a lot of money for it. He buys a Mercedes-Benz, a Saab 9000 CD or a Rolls Royce. Any industry with a variety of competing goods and services can be classified in this way.

Customers in the upper left zone of the graph get more value than they pay for. They reckon they have got a bargain. Companies selling products in this zone usually increase their market shares. In actual fact, the value graph for any given industry must show a fairly uniform spread of products from different companies. Some must be regarded as better value for money than others.

A company whose products are in the bottom right zone of the graph is not so happily situated. Its product (goods and/or services) is not regarded as worth the asking price, and the customer reckons he is paying over the odds for what he is getting in return.

In the bottom right zone, I have drawn a point with two arrows pointing away from it. The classical strategy for a company finding itself in this position is to move leftward in the graph by rationalizing its costs and capital (managing its resources) to be able to cut its prices and thus be regarded as competitive.

There is however another possible way to get your product accepted as worth its price, and that is to move upward on the graph, to get your product back into the competitive band by increasing its customer-perceived value. The trouble with using the value variable is that it involves taking commercial risks and is difficult to model mathematically. The thinking needed to understand what customers perceive as valuable is also different from that needed for resource management.

Thinking on the subject of value goes a long way back. Aristotle drew attention to a problem with ethical overtones which has exercised economists for a very long time: 'Why should the most useful things in existence have the lowest market value, while some of the least useful command the highest prices?' Until well into the 19th Century, many economists were preoccupied with the distinction between usage value and exchange value. Bread and potable water are useful and relatively cheap, whereas silks and diamonds have little practical use but are far more expensive.

Adam Smith got stuck on the same question. The riddle of usage value and exchange value was not to be solved for another century or more until the discovery of marginal utility – one of the minor triumphs of economic science. This term refers to the fact that it is the most desirable usage that determines value. The utility value of water is marginal because of its abundance, and the value of diamonds is high because of their rarity. One could conceive of a situation in an arid desert where the brightest and most splendid of gems would gladly be exchanged for a glass of water. Scarcity creates value. Adam Smith solved this by what he called the labour theory of value, by which he simply meant that the value of an asset is measured by the amount of labour for which it can be exchanged.

The classical economists approached the problem of value from the cost side, proposing costs of labour as the explanation of the value of anything. The neo-classicists, on the other hand, held that it was utility that determined value quantitatively and was actually the key factor in explaining the system of micro-economic relations.

The theory of marginal utility, like many conceptual breakthroughs, arose at about the same time in a large number of places when the time was ripe for its acceptance. The economist to whom the development of the theory was attributed was Herman Heinrich Gossen (1810–58). Gossen expounded his theory in a book which, unfortunately, did not sell very well. So he himself collected the remaindered copies, made a bonfire of them and died a disappointed and embittered man, totally unaware of his posthumous fame.

The essence of marginal utility theory can be expressed thus: 'The marginal utility of an article is the increment to total utility or satisfaction generated by the most recently purchased unit of the article in question' (Richard T. Gill, *Modern Economics*).

There are also two important corollaries to the theory:

1 The law of diminishing marginal utility states that marginal utility to the consumer diminishes with increasing consumption of a given product.
2 The consumer tends to maximize the total utility of his/her consumption by distributing purchases of goods in such a way that the marginal utility of buying one type of goods is equal to the marginal utility of buying any other type of goods.

This theory of value thus has much in common with the general law of supply and demand.

There are plenty of examples of companies that have concentrated too hard on rationalizing their costs. The EXPERIENCE CURVE precept that doubled production saves about 20 per cent in unit costs has created a predilection for high-volume production and low unit costs despite the fact that they detract from the creation of value.

Example 1

The Swedish Consumer Co-operative Movement has merged co-op societies, utilized economies of scale in its distribution depots and all its other facilities that supply goods to its retail outlets, and pursued the goal of rationalization in general ever since the mid-1970s. Throughout that period its market shares have steadily dwindled, because it has failed to do anything about the value variable, the pleasure associated with shopping.

Example 2

An airline bought four wide-bodied Airbus aircraft, mainly to reduce the cost per passenger seat on its high-frequency, short-haul routes. It seemed a sensible idea to replace a number of DC9 departures with a smaller number of Airbus departures, which meant that more passengers could be carried per flight at a lower cost per head. Unfortunately the rationale of this idea collided with customer-perceived value because the longer intervals between departures reduced travellers' freedom of choice.

Example 3

General Motors was formed in 1908 by a number of car manufacturers who were in danger of being driven to the wall by Ford's production rationale: 'You can have any colour you like as long as it's black.' That statement, attributed to Henry Ford, represented the triumph of rational production over customers' needs. The reason why Ford used black paint was that it dried fast and did not slow down production on the endless belt.

The GM management under Alfred P. Sloan coined a new corporate mission at the beginning of the 1930s: 'We will make a car for every need and every wallet.' This commitment to differentiation, to different products for different customer needs, almost put Ford out of business.

Now, half a century later, GM has its troubles. The corporation has been sued by a number of car owners who had bought Buicks and discovered the name Chevrolet stamped on the engines. Having paid for Buicks, they were not satisfied with Chevrolet engines.

GM has fallen into the same trap that Ford fell into in the 1920s. It has carried rational production so far that it has eroded the customer-perceived value of differentiation, because its cars are too much alike.

These three examples illustrate the danger of concentrating too much on rationalizing resources and going to extremes in the pursuit of volume production and low unit costs. The art of modern management is of course to strike an optimum balance between rational use of resources on the one hand and customer-perceived value on the other.

The value variable is much more complex than it appears at first sight. Behind customer-perceived value lie need structures whose nature can be extremely subtle.

Only about 20 per cent of all purchases of personal computers can be justified by rational cost-benefit calculations. In nearly 80 per cent of cases, the purchase is prompted by non-rational motives, according to a survey made by Apple Computers in the United States. A company that had a batch of PCs warming its shelves tarted up the casings and jacked up the price by a large percentage, whereupon they soon cleared the stock. The need structure that underlies the buying of a PC is very often the need to demonstrate professional success. In satisfying that need, PCs compete with turbo-charged cars, car telephones and Armani suits.

The subtle components of the value variable are hard for rationally schooled people to understand, but they are perhaps one of the most important ingredients of businessmanship.

The problem in achieving a holistic view of business that includes an understanding of customer-perceived value is that it requires a different set of personal qualities than those needed for rational management of resources. Intelligence, education and analytical ability are not enough. You must also possess empathy, the ability to put yourself in the other fellow's place. You must be interested in customers at the micro level and have an instinctive understanding of the value judgments that prompt their choice of suppliers.

VERTICAL INTEGRATION

Vertical integration means that market transactions are replaced by in-house transactions.

Vertical integration, like diversification, was at one time the height of fashion in business management, although it passed its peak of popularity some decades ago. A classic example is Singer, the American sewing machine company that at one period integrated its total operations from primary raw material sources (forests and iron mines) to finished sewing machines. Most industries have now been through a phase of diminishing integration in that they are making less of the end product themselves and buying more components from outside suppliers.

In theory, all functions can be operated as separate companies. You can hive off a computer department, a factory, a sales company and other parts of the administrative apparatus. A decision on vertical integration is essentially a decision whether to make products and provide services yourself or buy them from somebody else.

These decisions are akin to establishment decisions and are based on the question of whether it is more profitable to make or buy. But the decision is of course not only a question of profitability but also, to a high degree, of strategy.

The disadvantages of advanced vertical integration have become increasingly apparent with time. Advanced vertical integration is a problem that troubles the directors of General Motors in Detroit. GM is the most vertically integrated of all the world's car manufacturers. In-house products and services account for about 65 per cent of the value of a finished GM car. The final drives, gearboxes and engines are all manufactured in GM's own plants. This has led to over-confidence in economies of scale, and has landed GM with some lawsuits from customers who have bought Buicks only to discover that the bonnets concealed Chevrolet engines. Those buyers were not prepared to accept a Chevrolet engine in a Buick. GM got itself into that situation by sacrificing differentiation on the altar of rational production. The result was that customer-perceived value suffered, and market shares with it.

A general observation, then, is that market transactions are much more efficient than in-house transactions. That is why companies are cutting their staff, because they have found that they can develop more effectively and improve their productivity by buying services from outside. Organizations of a centralistic nature tend to have a misplaced faith in their own abilities, which is expressed in a desire to do everything themselves.

More entrepreneurially inclined organizations, on the other hand, show the reverse tendency, making the whole chain more efficient by buying what they need from other companies.

The disadvantages of advanced vertical integration, which have become more and more evident as time goes on, are these:

1 It eliminates market forces, and with them their corrective effect on accumulation of deadwood.
2 It makes it tempting to introduce subsidies which distort the competitive picture and obscure the question of *raison d'être*.
3 It gives an artificial negotiating strength, which does not correspond to the reality of negotiations on a free market.
4 It creates mutual dependence, which can be a handicap to any of the functions involved if it runs into trouble.
5 The captive market (guaranteed outlet) which it creates lulls the organization into a false sense of security.
6 This false sense of security blunts the willingness and ability of the organization to compete.

Illusions

Even today, many cases of vertical integration are the result of self-deception or mistaken beliefs. The most usual fallacy is to believe that you can eliminate competition in a given step in the production chain by dominating it. Some of the illusions prevalent in the world of vertical integration are:

1 *A strong market position at one stage of production is transferable to another stage.* This belief has often led to bad investment decisions in the Swedish Consumer Co-operative movement and other conglomerates, which have subsequently been afflicted by all the disadvantages listed above.
2 *In-house trading cuts out salesmen, simplifies administration and therefore makes transactions cheaper.* This, of course, is nothing but the classic creed of the economic planner for whom central control is dogma and free market forces anathema.
3 *We can rescue a strategically weak unit by buying up the link before or after it in the production chain.* This may be feasible in exceptional cases, but they are rare. The logic of every industry must be judged on its own merits and that applies here too unless it is a case of diversification to spread risks.
4 *Knowledge of the industry can be utilized to gain a competitive edge in an upstream or downstream operation.* This may be true, but it is advisable

to scrutinize the alleged advantages closely to be sure that the logic is not fallacious.

There are plenty of examples of spectacular improvements in profitability achieved by breaking up vertically integrated structures. This is probably the reason why business as a whole is moving in the direction of less integration. Car makers with their own shipping lines do not deliver their cars to export markets more cheaply than those who use the services of independent shipping companies. Nor can they make their own gearboxes at lower cost than specialist gearbox manufacturers. The list of examples could be made very long.

One of the reasons why vertical integration was so popular during the technocratic era was, I think, the evident economies of scale which were tangible and computable, as opposed to the advantages of small scale, such as entrepreneurial spirit and competitive drive, which cannot be reduced to numbers.

There are also some definite advantages to vertical integration in certain special cases, especially where control of a key resource gives a competitive edge. In those cases, vertical integration is beneficial. Some of the advantages are:

- better co-ordination of operations with better possibilities for control
- closer contact with end users through forward integration
- access to technological know-how of crucial importance in a particular industry
- assured supply of essential products and services

A large European travel agency integrated into the hotel business by establishing holiday villages at tourist resorts. This is an example of expansion from selling package holidays to providing holiday accommodation, a step that was judged to offer a strategic advantage. United Airlines' investment in hotels is another example, and yet another is Ikea's backward integration from selling furniture into design and production planning, balanced by forward de-integration by leaving the last step in production, assembly of the furniture, to the customers themselves.

Vertical integration is often prompted by motives of self-aggrandizement or overweening pride, so it is advisable to examine your own motives if you are contemplating it.

VISION

Vision is the term used to describe a picture of a relatively remote future in which business has developed under the best possible conditions and in accordance with the hopes and dreams of the owner or chief executive. A vision provides a benchmark for what one hopes to achieve in business, and can be a guide to the level of ambition of strategic planning.

A more detailed discussion will be found under the entry GOALS AND VISIONS.

Models

BCG MATRIX

One of the most important developments in the evolution of strategy was the introduction of the two-dimensional matrix. The first of these matrices to come into wide use was the Boston (Mass.) Consulting Group's Growth/Share Matrix.

To use the BCG Matrix, you plot the growth rate of a business unit's market on one axis (usually the vertical one) against the business unit's share of that market on the other axis.

Most analysts consider absolute market share to be of secondary importance in this context, preferring to take the market share of the two to four largest competitors as the baseline. Relative market share is thus the most usual yardstick.

The real usefulness of the BCG Matrix lay in using it to plot the relative positions of business units within a portfolio. This made it possible to identify winners (market leaders) and to determine whether a balance existed between units in the four quadrants. The theory is that business units in fast-growing industries need a constant input of capital to enable them to expand their capacity. Business units in slow-growing industries, on the other hand, are expected to generate a positive cash flow.

This matrix was used chiefly as a way to assess the need for financing in diversified corporations. It did not attempt to explain the criteria for success or the state of competition in different industries, but was intended simply to help the managements of diversified groups manage their portfolios. Large corporations have a need to balance their portfolios by mixing business units that need capital to grow with units that generate capital.

This matrix undoubtedly owes much of its popularity to the names given to the four quadrants:

1 Business units with a large market share in growth sectors are called stars.

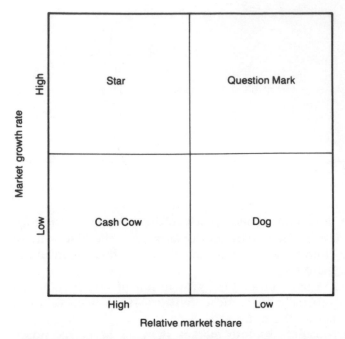

Figure 25 The BCG Growth/Share Matrix. It aroused great interest when it was first published.

2 Units with a high market share in well-established industries are called cash cows.
3 Units with small market shares in fast-growing industries are called question marks (or mavericks).
4 Units with a low market share in a stagnant market are called dogs.

The BCG Matrix has subsequently come in for some hard, and to some extent justified, criticism. All attempts at model construction necessarily involve a skilful choice of simplifications, but in the light of today's knowledge the simplifications in the BCG Matrix look far too sweeping.

BUSINESS CYCLE

The structure shown in figure 26 has proved to be a highly instructive way of making basic business relationships clear.

Marketing can be equated with creation of demand. Profit is often the same thing as return on resources. By resources we mean here not only costs and capital but also immaterial resources in the form of know-how and special skills.

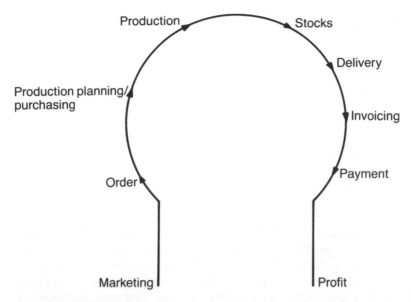

Figure 26 The Business Cycle. Its graphic illustration helps to clarify the basic principles of business.

The Business Cycle is closely associated with the four basic functions of business management: development, production, marketing and administration. The value of this simple type of structure is that it helps to give a clear picture of complex organizational and business structures. In the Business Cycle it is the interactions between these functions to which special attention must be paid in the design and staffing of organizations. Each function in the Business Cycle can in turn be broken down into sub-functions. Every company has broad functions, like personnel and management.

To complete the association we can add to figure 26, under 'marketing', the needs of individuals and legal entities. We can also add the need for return on capital, which in its turn satisfies a number of motives in a motivation system.

ELEMENTS OF STRATEGY

In conjunction with strategy development processes, I have felt a strong need to strengthen strategic thinking with reference to the implementation process. For this purpose I have found it useful to specify nine key variables that influence the way a company or business unit deploys its resources. I call these variables the elements of strategy.

These elements, taken together, provide an excellent indication of how a company or business unit is using and marshalling its resources to move in a given direction. Taken together, the nine elements give a very clear picture of the way a company or business unit is using and concentrating its resources.

1 *Corporate mission*

The concept of corporate mission represents the opportunity that exists on a market to satisfy defined needs by supplying a given product to a given category of customers in competition with a given group of competitors. Corporate missions have a tendency to age, which often gives rise to uncertainty about the means of competition and the product.

It is usually fairly easy to tell how clear a strategy is by noting how the management of a company defines its corporate mission. There is a tendency to stagnate in old, well-worn patterns when it comes to reinterpreting the needs that lie behind actual demand and the changing patterns of need structures. Demand is subject to constantly changing influences, for example when competitors develop new products and new technology. The underlying needs are usually fairly constant, while demand shifts towards the product that best satisfies those needs.

2 *Competitive edge*

Perhaps the most important element of strategy is the choice of how to compete. The purpose of strategy can be expressed as achieving a higher degree of need satisfaction than the competition can achieve, and thereby attaining a position that will generate a rate of profit above the average for the industry. The aim of securing a competitive edge is intimately associated with the choice of markets and adjustment of the product, for example, but it can also affect the structure of investments. If you choose a strategy aimed at getting a cost advantage through efficient production, it will mainly affect production structures, investment, and development projects concerned with the economics of production. In mass markets with few opportunities for product differentiation, the competitive edge chosen will not be the same as in a market where there is more scope for varying the product.

3 *Business organization*

Business organization refers to the way an organization subdivides itself for business purposes. Almost every company has an organization that is differentiated on the basis of products, product groups, customers or markets. Part of a company's strategy is thus reflected in how its business organization is first differentiated and then reintegrated. If, for example, you are selling Renault products in Norway or Canada, you will probably segment your external market between trucks and cars. You will then integrate the business in a national sales company, which in turn represents a differentiation on a geographical basis. Then you integrate that into a regional organization on the one hand and a product organization on the other.

4 *Product*
Product is used here as a generic term for goods and services. It may be difficult to form a complete picture of how well a product matches the structure of customers' needs, but you should make a real effort to do so. One way is to find out whether the company has made any recent attempt to check its product against customers' needs. You can also check up on how much of your turnover comes from new products and services, to get an idea of how the total product is evolving. Yet another idea is to consider how a hardware-producing company has built up services to support its hardware.

5 *Markets*
Markets are not defined by geography alone, but also by the application or use of the product. You may, for example, want to sell to certain segments in a niche in which you think the pressure of competition will be less.

The infinite corporate mission is to sell everything to everybody everywhere. In your strategy development you have to narrow down that limitless vista according to your corporate mission so that you can concentrate your energies on the customers you most want to sell to. The apparently obvious step of defining primary target groups is often neglected, yet it is one of the most essential elements of strategy.

6 *Resources*
Resources in this context comprise investments and costs. Investments are usually channelled to support the strategy, and their nature says a lot about a company's dominant value judgments and strategies. In the case of an airline, for example, you can note whether it has put most of its investment into buying new aircraft or upgrading its personnel and range of services. If you find a shipping company that has invested in real estate over a long period of time, that says something about its strategies just as much as if it had invested in new ships. Development of markets, personnel and other software can also be regarded as investments. The orientation of the whole cost complex is a decisive element of strategy.

7 *Structural changes*

Structural changes, or the buying and selling of business units, are also significant indicators of a company's strategic philosophy. Initiatives for structural change are seldom taken at the business unit level. It is particularly unusual for the head of a business unit to suggest that his unit should be sold to another group of owners. The reason is probably that any such suggestion would be ill received by the present owners. Structural changes naturally offer strong clues to a company's view of its own future.

8 *Development programmes*

Development of products, markets, business and so on is usually a part of the total investment programme. Corporate R & D projects are, hopefully, the result of a strategic policy, whether prompted by technology-push or by market demand. Unfortunately it is not uncommon for a technological culture to acquire its own momentum and engage in development projects that are unrelated to business strategy. Development programmes are one of the clearest strategic indicators.

9 *Management competence and culture*

Management competence and culture are also strategic indicators. You should study how management operates, and especially to what extent entrepreneurship and drive are rewarded or penalized. The level of ambition is usually determined by top management, and it is a good idea to find out whether there is a level of ambition agreed upon by all the leading executives, or whether the subject has ever been discussed at all.

The degree of strategic leadership ability is naturally just as important. The company's corporate mission, goals and strategies are interesting questions to raise. It is easy to judge the level of strategic leadership ability from the answers. The level may in fact be high, even if the answers do not trip freely off the tongue.

The concept of corporate culture includes a number of basic value judgments that are expressed in various ways. Some of them are:

- attitude to risk-taking in business
- acceptance of the entrepreneurial spirit, of high performance motivation and low relation orientation
- attitudes to quality and customer satisfaction
- attitudes to people, customers and employees
- attitudes to work, success and failure

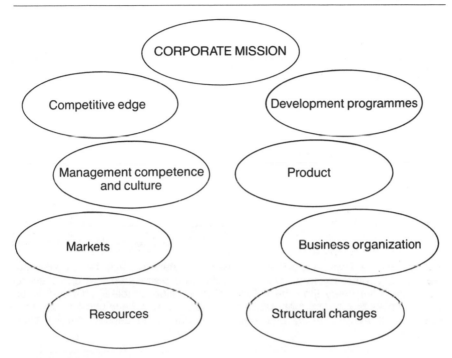

Figure 27 Elements of strategy. Nine key factors that control the way a company or business unit uses its resources.

EXPERIENCE CURVE

The Experience Curve says that any operation in a production process can be performed at about 20 per cent lower unit cost if the volume is doubled. This theory is the basis of many of the older strategy models, including the BCG Matrix.

The Experience Curve, which dates back to 1926, is mainly applicable to manufacturing operations. It is classic in so far as it constitutes the essence of the economy-of-scale philosophy that long dominated strategy development.

The theory implies that a large market share is valuable because it offers opportunities to increase production capacity and thus move down the Experience Curve in the direction of lower production costs. In this way you can achieve higher margins, better profitability and, consequently, a better competitive position.

It further implies that accumulated production makes it possible to benefit from experience, which will gradually improve the efficiency of production. There is a constant teaching effect in addition to the opportunities to specialize and distribute capital costs over a larger number of manufactured units.

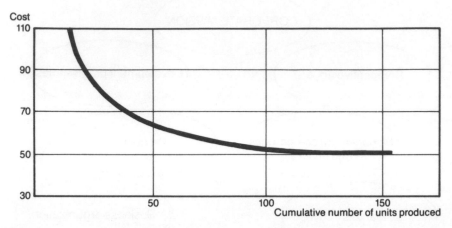

Figure 28 The Experience Curve. It was invented in 1926 by an American officer. With reference to aircraft construction, he discovered that unit costs fell by 20 per cent every time the volume of production doubled. This correlation, which applies to physical manufacturing operations, has since come to dominate business strategy thinking and has, for example, influenced market share theories.

Explanation of the Experience Curve

The effects of the Experience Curve are not based on a natural law, so it is necessary to understand the causes that produce the effects. The cost reductions which are a consequence of the correlation do not occur automatically; the possibilities must be known and actively exploited. The underlying phenomena overlap and are strongly inter-related, but they can be analytically distinguished, which we shall now do.

Efficiency of labour: when workers repeat a given task, they do so with progressively greater efficiency. Wastage is reduced, and productivity increases. This process can be accelerated by training and wise per-sonnel management policies.

Organization of work: adjustment of work organization may manifest itself in two ways. The degree of specialization may increase with rising volume, or the organization may be restructured to match the flow of production more closely. In the former case this means that each worker performs fewer tasks. The latter is exemplified by the Swedish car industry, which has shown how production flows can be altered.

New production process: inventions and improvements in the pro-duction process can play a significant part in reducing unit costs, especially in capital-intensive industries.

Balance of labour and capital: as a business develops, the balance between labour and capital may change. If wages rise, for example, money may be diverted from wages to investment in robots. This has happened in countries with high labour costs like Japan, Sweden and the old Federal Republic of Germany.

Standardization of products: the benefits of the Experience Curve cannot be utilized to the full without standardization of production. Ford's production of their Model T in the 1920s is an example of how standardization can lead to a dangerous lack of flexibility. Thus standardized mass production tends to inhibit innovation in a company.

Technical specialization: as the production process develops, specialized equipment may be procured which results in more efficient production and thus in reduced costs.

Design modifications: as experience accumulates, both customers and manufacturer acquire greater knowledge of the relationship between price and performance. Through value engineering, products can be redesigned to save material, energy and labour while maintaining or improving performance.

Economies of scale: from the analytical standpoint, economies of scale are actually a separate phenomenon that may occur independently of the Experience Curve. The overlap, however, is so great that economies of scale must be noted as an essential factor, even though their effects on the Experience Curve may be comparatively small. A company with a high volume of production can not only derive greater benefit from economies of scale, but can also move along the Experience Curve farther and faster than smaller companies in its industry as a result of the sheer volume effect.

GAP ANALYSIS

GAP analysis was developed at the Stanford Research Institute in California. It can be characterized as an attempt to find a method of dealing with strategy development and managing one's way to a higher level of ambition.

The steps in a GAP analysis are given below. This particular example refers to a portfolio analysis, that is to a group of business units, but similar schemes have also been developed for dealing with individual business units.

1 Formulate preliminary performance goals for one year, three years and five years.
2 Forecast profit development relative to currently set goals for existing business units.

3 Establish gap between goals and forecasts.
4 Identify other investment alternatives for each business unit and forecast results.
5 Identify general alternative competitive positions for each business unit and forecast results.
6 Discuss investments and business strategy alternatives for each business unit.
7 Arrive at synthesis of the portfolio perspective with reference to goal strategy for each business unit.
8 Establish gap between preliminary performance target and forecast for each business unit.
9 Specify profile of possible business unit acquisitions.
10 Determine resources required to make such acquisitions and effect on existing business units.
11 Revise goals and strategies of existing business units with a view to creating these resources.
12 Establish a synthesis that determines goals and strategies.

GAP analysis can thus be described as an organized attack on the gap between desired and predicted performance.

LOTS

When discussing VALUE we briefly discussed the problem of a holistic view of business. We saw that rational and analytical evaluations are not enough; an ability to empathize with customers and others is often even more important.

A method attempting to integrate all the elements in a holistic view of business was developed around 1980. The method is called LOTS, which is the Swedish word for pilot.

LOTS was first applied in an analysis of the market potential of hyaluric acid (cockscomb extract). As a result of the analysis, marketing efforts were concentrated on eye surgery, one of dozens of theoretically possible applications. That was the origin of Pharmacia's most profitable operation: the product, under the brand name Healon, has revolutionized modern eye surgery.

The LOTS business language has since been systematized in seminar form. It has been taught to executives in Swedish business and foreign subsidiaries of Swedish companies, as well as to Japanese, Australian, American and Canadian businessmen. A somewhat abbreviated version is studied by people not directly involved in customer contacts or marketing. In-house coaches run follow-up courses within companies and refine the application of the method.

The basic philosophy of LOTS is that a company, government

agency or other organization ought to be suffused with the desire and ability to adapt its operations to its customers' requirements. Both private business and public administration are so complex today that an in-depth understanding of the environment in which they operate is essential to an appreciation of customers' wishes and motives. Thinking must proceed from the outside inward.

It sounds simple. Most people, in their own opinion, are already doing just that. It has been found, however, that rigorous application of the LOTS principle leads to great changes in the way the company operates.

The method as such comprises a sequence of questions to be discussed in detail. The sequence can be applied to business problems on various levels and of various degrees of complexity, from the corporate mission of a whole company to an individual project within one unit. The quality of the discussion determines how successful the LOTS approach will be.

The sequence contains nine steps: objective, strategies, long-term goals, short-term goals, activities, personnel analysis, development plans, organization, and reporting.

Different business strategy models and problem solutions can be used to go through the nine steps. The aim is to create an overview that will guide the company, unit or individual along the right path in relation to the outside world.

MCKINSEY'S 7S MODEL

McKinsey's 7S Model cannot really be considered as a pure strategy model, but rather as a way of thinking about development or remodelling of organizations. Its name comes from the seven factors that McKinsey found essential in the context of organization development: strategy, skills, shared values, structure, systems, staff, and style.

Normally, when a company sets out to change its organization, the seven S's are dealt with in a given sequence. In the first phase the strategy is usually determined. The next step is to define what the organization must be specially good at in order to be able to implement its strategy, in other words, what skills it must develop or otherwise acquire. The final step is to determine what changes are needed in the other five factors to make the change a successful one.

Strategy describes where the company or business unit should concentrate its forces and compete, and what co-ordinated actions must be taken to achieve a sustained competitive edge. Strategy, in other words, answers the questions of where the company should compete and how.

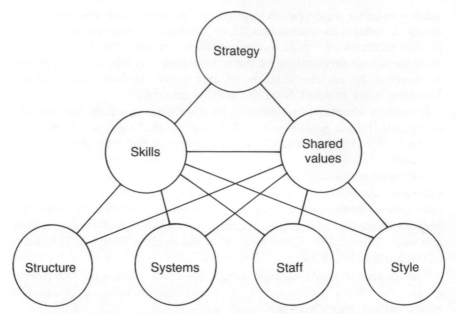

Figure 29 McKinsey's 7S Model. McKinsey lists seven essential factors in organization development and shows how they are linked.

Source Dag Sundström, McKinsey & Company Inc., Stockholm

Assuming that one has a clear idea of a suitable strategy for the company, the next step is to decide what essential organizational skills the new strategy calls for.

The strategy tells the company how it must adapt itself to its environment and use its organizational potential, whereas the analysis of skills answers the question of how the strategy ought to be implemented.

It is seldom difficult to define five, or maybe even ten skills of fundamental importance. But this is not enough, because the need is to develop winning skills and this often makes such heavy demands on the organization that it is only possible to develop between one and three skills at a time. These skills represent the link between the strategy and the new era, while at the same time they define the changes that need to be made in the other five S's: structure, systems, staff, style and shared values.

A company's structure is perhaps the best known of the concepts relating to organizational change. It refers to the way business areas, divisions and units are grouped in relation to each other. This, too, is perhaps the most visible factor in the organization, and that is why it is often tempting to begin by changing the structure. There are many examples of corporate managements who thought they could reorganize their companies through structural changes alone.

Systems can be defined as the routines or processes which exist in a company and which involve many people for the purpose of identifying important issues, getting things done or making decisions. Systems have a very strong influence on what happens in most organizations, and provide management with a powerful tool for making changes in the organization.

The staff factor is concerned with the question of what kind of people the company needs. This is not so much a question of single individuals as of the total know-how possessed by the people in the organization.

Style is one of the lesser-known implements in the management tool-box. It can be said to consist of two elements: personal style and symbolic actions. Thus management style is not a matter of personal style but of what the executives in the organization do: how do they use their personal signal system?

Shared values, finally, refer to one or more guiding themes of the organization, things that everybody is aware of as being specially important and crucial to the survival and success of the organization.

As we have seen, skills are the integrating factor in the 7S Model. According to this model, when you think of organizational change you start by thinking about strategy, and on the basis of that strategy you define the most important skills you need before proceeding to decide what changes are necessary in the other factors in the 7S Model.

The 7S Model has often been misinterpreted, and has consequently been applied in an imprecise fashion. This model does not in fact pretend to be a guide to the development of either business or portfolio strategies, but simply represents a holistic view of corporate development. The fact that some people are put off by acronyms should not be allowed to obscure the model's explanatory value.

MARKET ANALYSES

The boundary between models and tools is sometimes blurred. All organized activity is designed to satisfy somebody's needs. This has given market analysis a new and much more important role in that it has become less manipulative, i.e. aimed not so much at selling an existing product range as at determining the underlying needs of potential customers. It is necessary to establish how well the company's products or services are capable of satisfying customer's needs.

I have therefore chosen to include three analytical instruments developed by B2B, a consultant firm belonging to the Scandstrat Group: positioning analysis, internal analysis and loyalty analysis. A similar approach can also be used for other forms of organizational diagnosis.

Positioning analysis

The first step in a positioning analysis is to try to identify the demands that customers make on a company's products or services and ask customers to rank them in order of importance. In the next step, customers are asked what they think of the company's ability to satisfy these demands. The analysis is made for all relevant companies in the industry.

Comparison with competitors is essential to the interpretation and strategic application of the information. We need to identify our strong points (which must be defended) as well as competitors' weak points (which should be attacked). Most important of all are our weak points, which must be strengthened. This is how we interpret Figure 30:

1 Characteristics in quadrant A are things which customers regard as important and which the company does well. It is these character-istics that have established the company's position, and they must be maintained.

2 Characteristics in quadrant B are things that the company is good at, but which are not so important. If the competition is just as good in quadrant A but our own company is better on some point in quadrant B, that point may tip the scale in the customer's choice of supplier. We may also get the effect of 'a little thing that makes a good company better'. So the added value of an advantage here may be important after all.

3 Quadrant C contains things which the company does not do well, but which do not matter so much to customers.

4 Quadrant D contains important things that the company does *not* do well. Attitudes need to be changed by advertising and/or product development. But remember that the product is a better measure of the value of advertising than *vice versa*. Your target group will only take so much on trust. It is seldom enough to claim that you are good: you must be able to prove it.

A positioning analysis can work like this: you want to know how important price, service, the technical features of your product, etc. are to success in the market-place. Enter the percentage of customers who say that price is decisive or important to their choice of supplier on the *Importance* axis. Then plot the percentage (out of those who consider price important) who are satisfied with the company's price level on the *Performance* axis.

Importance

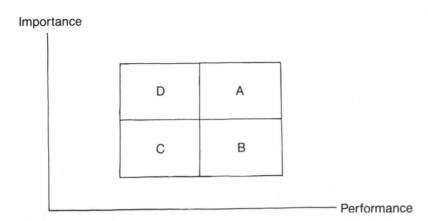

Performance

Figure 30 Positioning analysis.

Internal analysis

It takes a confrontation between internal beliefs and outside reality (i.e. the market) to make people inside an organization realize and accept the need for change. This can be done by getting salespeople, marketing staff and management to say how they think customers have answered the questions in the positioning analysis. The object of this exercise is to determine:

- whether the organization is under/overestimating itself
- whether it is under/overestimating its competitors
- what market demands it attaches too much/too little importance to

Results could be arranged thus:

Result: market needs
We have underestimated the importance of certain factors.

Consequence
We have failed to stress these factors enough in our sales work because we did not think they mattered.

We have overestimated the importance of certain factors.

We thought these were the reasons why customers buy our products, but they are not

Result: own position
We have overrated our own relative performance, believing ourselves to be best.

Consequence
We have not bothered about our competitors, taking it for granted that the market recognizes our superiority.

| We have underrated our own performance. | We have been too timid in our stance in the market-place and have failed to take advantage of our opportunities. |

Loyalty analysis – market position

A company is constantly exposed to comparison, and if it fails to satisfy the demands of the market it will be dropped. A fall-off in customer loyalty is an early warning that something is wrong.

A strong market position is the result of ability to penetrate the market and secure the loyalty of customers. The analysis can be made like this. The market is polled to find out about:

- penetration for each of the actors, i.e. the percentage of customers who buy from each company
- success in winning customer loyalty, i.e. how much of the customer's needs the company supplies

Examples of positions of a company and its competitors include:

1 High penetration (100 per cent) and high loyalty. This company is the market leader (quadrant A in Figure 31).
2 Lower penetration and lower loyalty. This is the traditional chief competitor. Sometimes the competitor commands a higher degree of loyalty, in which case we are only 'second best' to our customers (quadrant B).
3 Low penetration and low loyalty. Not much danger from these competitors – mainly marginal purchases (quadrant C).
4 Low penetration but high loyalty, i.e. the few who have bought from this company have been impressed. This company has potential – the opportunity to steal customers from the market leader. It is necessary to detect this in time to be able to determine the reason. Is it a company likely to expand in the future, or has it simply found a niche that does not match the profile our own company wants to display? The important thing is to identify, analyse, decide what to do and possibly make changes (quadrant D).

MARKET ECONOMY vs. PLANNED ECONOMY

In the 1990s market economy has won a total victory in its world-wide struggle against planned economy. A need has therefore arisen to explain the differences between the ways in which market economy and planned economy work.

It is widely believed that market economy is synonymous with

Loyalty

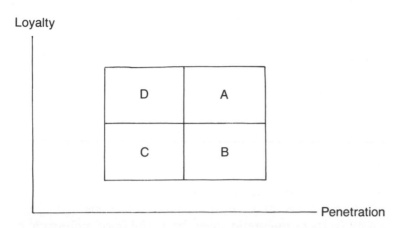

Penetration

Figure 31 Loyalty analysis. The market leader is in quadrant A. It sells to many customers, and they are loyal to it. The losers are to be found in quadrants B and C, where B represents a serious competitor who cannot command the same loyalty, and C is the anonymous company whose customers are few and casual. The potential future market leader is in quadrant D, with loyal customers who are willing to buy more.

capitalism. Although the two nearly always coincide, analytically they are two different things. Capitalism is simply another term for private ownership. It is quite possible to conceive State capitalism with market economy. This would be an economy in which the State owns all the companies, but free-market conditions prevail in the form of profitability criteria, Darwinistic survival of the fittest and closure of unprofitable companies. Market economy means, quite simply, that an assortment of goods and services is produced to satisfy a demand which, through a series of individual decisions, determines what is sold and thus what is produced.

Companies always strive to attract customers and influence demand in favour of their own products by offering the best value in terms of the relationship between quality and price. This leads to competition between companies.

The essence of market economy is expressed in the value graph on page, where quality is plotted along the vertical axis and price along the horizontal axis. Quality reflects the value that customers pay for, while price is controlled by the resources (costs and capital) that the producer must use in order to be able to offer a given value.

To simplify somewhat, we can say that market economies always strive for an optimum combination of rational resource management and customer-perceived quality, whereas planned economies concentrate almost exclusively on rational resource management.

Let us characterize the two economic systems as they would be presented by adherents expounding their respective merits.

Planned economy

The blessings of planned economy can be summarized as follows:

1 Production can be planned ideally. Output is regulated by the production process instead of production having to be adapted to demand. This gives a high degree of rationality in production.

2 Transaction costs are substantially lower. By eliminating market transactions and leaving only internal transactions to be made, we can draw up long-term agreements that do away with the time-consuming negotiations involved in market transactions.

3 The chain of vertical integration can be maintained unbroken in combines and suchlike organizations, from ear of corn to loaf of bread, with a minimum of selling processes and transportation of goods.

4 Production can be rationalized to the ultimate, thus generating the effects of the Experience Curve. Long production runs become possible, leading to economies of scale in all functions.

5 Aside from production, advantages are also achieved on the development side because there is no need to develop numerous variants side by side. A few models suffice, enabling production apparatus to be utilized rationally and eliminating duplication of development costs.

6 The huge over-capacity that characterizes the distribution networks of market economies can be avoided. It has been calculated that the retail trade has a surplus capacity of 400 to 500 per cent. Planned economy does away with this extremely wasteful state of affairs.

7 The planned-economy route to efficiency involves utilizing extremely rational production management to produce goods cheaply. Quality and value to the user are not controlling factors, nor are they regarded as essential. The important thing is to satisfy the people's need for a good basic product or service.

Planned economy has an irresistible fascination for educated people who have been trained in deductive thinking throughout their education. Exactly the same phenomenon is found in large corporations and the public sector in Western countries. An attitude commonly found in large corporations is illustrated by the following quotations:

- 'We must avoid internal competition'.
- 'We must concentrate our resources'.

- 'Why should we buy this part from somebody else when we can make it ourselves?'

In planned economic systems there is no pressure from demand. This leads to technocratization of management (a technocrat is a person whose approach to technical or economic problems is strictly rational, with no allowance made for human values). The technocratic style of management is marked by a high degree of self sufficiency, i.e. a desire to do as much as possible oneself without help from others.

This is particularly well exemplified by municipal authorities in Sweden, who have long since integrated their operations horizontally and vertically to the point where they are nowadays involved in numerous activities which are of no strategic value whatsoever to their taxpayers.

The seductiveness of planned economy lies in its outward appearance of rationality. Efficient production, low transaction costs and control of complex systems are prospects that appeal primarily to power-oriented people. It is therefore difficult for individuals schooled in planned economy to understand the apparent chaos that prevails in market economies.

Rationality in production is limited by a number of *diseconomies* of scale which are seldom spoken of. They include:

1 Compromise.
2 Lack of flexibility.
3 Co-ordination mania.

Rationality in production and the possibility of planning complex systems in detail are the essence of planned economy thinking. This contrasts with the market-economy emphasis on customer-perceived value and the Darwinistic nature of large systems, or what Josef Schumpeter called 'creative destruction', meaning that inefficient systems should be allowed to perish and make way for new and more efficient structures.

Market economy

Market economy is based on a combination of creating value for customers and using production resources rationally. High quality and high value are generated by a will to innovate. Creativity, the combination of known elements in new ways, is one of the key factors in a company that operates in a market economy.

Let us, as before, describe market economy as one of its adherents might do:

1 Customers and markets, not central bureaucrats, decide what constitutes value.
2 Market economy promotes efficiency. Efficiency means high value
  at low cost in terms of resource consumption. Unlike planned economy, market economy strives both to enhance customer-perceived
  value and to reduce costs through rational production and in other
  ways.
3 Market economy promotes pluralism, which makes life more enjoy-
  able. The opposite of variety is monotony.
4 Market economy stimulates competition between companies, which
  gives them an inducement to satisfy their customers and minimize
  their costs. This leads to natural selection of the companies that
  perform best.
5 The value-creating aspect makes innovation and creativity important
  elements in market economy.

Market economy has proved its superiority to planned economy in
terms of creating high value at low cost, i.e. it has proved more
efficient. Nevertheless, numerous planned economic systems still sur-
vive in areas where major gains in social efficiency stand to be made.
This applies mainly to the welfare state systems that exist in Europe
and perhaps most of all in Scandinavia, where great gains in efficiency
are possible.

In a market economy the channelling of resources between different
sectors of society likewise takes place largely on the basis of market
demand. However, we find constraints upon the functioning of market
economy in almost every country, for example in health care and
education. Characteristically, it is the planned economy systems in
Western countries that have the greatest problems with efficiency.

One of the principal motives for official control of social resources
that are not controlled by demand is that people do not perceive the
need for them all the time, but only sporadically. We do not feel a
need for medical care until we fall ill; the need for education is a
matter of equality of opportunity; and so on.

To sum up, we can note some fundamental differences between
planned and market economies:

1 Planned economies set goals strictly in terms of rational production,
  not efficiency in the form of better quality.
2 Where customers have no choice, as is the case in planned economies, companies have no inducement to produce rationally either.
  As a result, planned economy results in production of poor quality
  at high cost.
3 The Darwinistic selection process which Josef Schumpeter called
  Creative Destruction is suppressed in planned economies. There is

no competition, so no effort is made to satisfy customers' needs at the lowest possible cost.

4 Planned economy presents a deceptive appearance of rationality in the form of economies of scale, no duplication of resources in the development and distribution functions, etc. In the long run, this inhibits productivity and innovation.

Let us conclude by citing the example of the US Air Force, which has introduced market economy into its procurement of combat aircraft. Instead of concentrating resources and pouring development resources into one organization, it orders prototypes from, say, four different companies. Although the development of these prototypes is expensive, at the end of the day the Air Force has four excellent aircraft to choose from.

The reader who wishes to pursue this subject further should study competition theory, which is an extended branch of economic science.

MARKET ATTRACTIVENESS AND STRATEGIC POSITION

Methods of rating market attractiveness and strategic position vary somewhat. The concept illustrated below was developed at roughly the same time by both the McKinsey Company and General Electric within the framework of the PIMS model (*see* PROFIT IMPACT OF MARKETING STRATEGY). Unlike the BCG MATRIX, this concept aimed at a more considered assessment of the prospects of individual business units. Figure 32 shows a matrix of this kind as used by McKinsey.

A special and very fundamental question is of course on what geographical market the relative market share should be calculated. There are plenty of examples on record of how misjudgments of market shares have led to disastrously bad decisions.

Some of the criteria used to judge strategic position and market attractiveness are:

Strategic position
- relative size
- growth
- market share
- position
- relative profitability
- margin
- technological position
- image (reality as perceived by out siders)
- leadership and people

Market attractiveness
- absolute size
- market growth
- market breadth
- pricing
- structure of competition
- industry profitability
- technical role
- social role
- effect on environment
- legal obstacles

These matrices have lately been very severely criticized. The criticism has focused mainly on the consequences of the recommendations that generally emanate from use of these matrices.

For example, if a business unit is judged to be in a weak strategic position in an unattractive market, the theory says that it should be harvested, that is milked for every last drop of capital that can be wrung out of it, and then dropped.

Following this advice has repeatedly proved disastrous. In the first place, who wants to be head of a company scheduled for rape and murder? General Electric, where much of this kind of thinking originated, has now radically reappraised such broad recommendations. Manufacture of tramcars, electricity transmission and other operations held to be in a poor strategic position on unpromising markets have proved capable of achieving great successes where management did the opposite of what the model recommended. Thus, for example, the manufacture and sale of tramcars and underground railway systems has proved to have a great development potential, the simplistic recommendations of the model to the contrary notwithstanding.

MINTZBERG'S FIVE STRUCTURES

Henry Mintzberg is one of the organization researchers who have strongly influenced thought in the 1970s and 1980s. His thinking is based on the proposition that organizations contain a number of forces that interact dynamically to create various contours. Figure 33 shows the five principal structures postulated by Mintzberg and the characteristics of each type.

1 *Simple Structure*

The Simple Structure is characterized above all by what is missing in its development. It has little or no techno-structure, few people in support functions, minimum differentiation between units, and a low hierarchy of management. Very little of its behaviour is formalized and it makes hardly any use of planning, training or communications. It is primarily organic.

Co-ordination within the Simple Structure is mostly handled by direct supervision. The top person has power over all decisions. The structure often consists of an organic nucleus with one person in charge.

The environment of the Simple Structure tends to be both simple and dynamic. A simple environment can be grasped by one person, who is therefore able to make all the decisions. A dynamic environment calls for an organic structure, which is one of the characteristics of the Simple Structure.

The Simple Structure is often a transient phase in the development

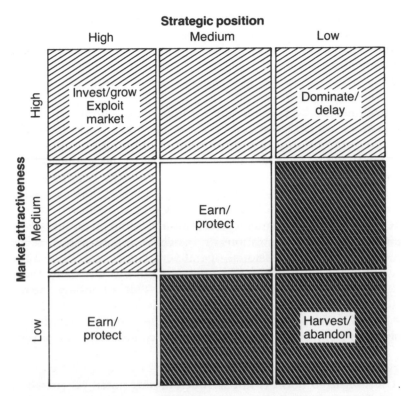

Strategic position

Figure 32 Market attractiveness and strategic position. McKinsey further developed the BCG Matrix in the course of a project commissioned by General Electric to create the McKinsey Matrix shown above. It takes more factors into account than the original Boston Matrix.

of an organization; as it grows, other forces come into play and call forth a different structure.

2 *Machine Bureaucracy*

A national postal service, a steelworks, a big car manufacturing company: all these organizations have a number of structural characteristics in common. Their operations are of a routine nature, often simple and repetitive, which results in heavily standardized procedures. These factors produce the Machine Bureaucracies in our society: structures that work like integrated, regulated machines.

The work done by the operative nucleus is here rationalized to the extreme and seldom calls for advanced training. The primary co-ordination mechanism is the standardization of work routines.

Because the Machine Bureaucracy relies so heavily on standardized routines, the techno-structure emerges as the most important aspect of this contour. It is manned by analysts who acquire great informal power, even though they are not part of the line organization, because they are the ones who standardize everybody else's work.

3 *Professional Bureaucracy*

Organizations can be bureaucratic without being centralized. These organizations are characterized by stable operative work that gives rise to predictable standardized behaviour. But they are also complex and must therefore be under the direct control of the operators who do the work. Because of this, structures of this kind resort to a co-ordination mechanism that simultaneously embraces both standardization and decentralization: standardization of know-how.

The Professional Bureaucracy, commonly found in universities, hospitals, school administrations and suchlike organizations, relies on the skills of its professional operatives. The organization hires highly educated specialists for its operative nucleus and gives them wide latitude to organize their own work. This autonomy means that the specialist works independently of his or her colleagues, but close to the customers he or she serves. A teacher, for example, is in sole charge of her classroom and in close contact with her pupils.

4 *Divisionalized Form*

The Divisionalized Form is not so much an integrated organization as a number of quasi-autonomous units linked by a central administration. Its units are usually called divisions (possibly organized as subsidiary companies), while the central administration is known as the Head Office.

Divisions are created to correspond to the markets the business wants to serve, and are given control of the operative functions needed to provide service to those markets. Separation of operative functions makes the units mutually independent, enabling each one to operate as an autonomous unit that is not required to co-ordinate with the others.

Decentralization in the Divisionalized Form is fairly limited. It need go no further than the executives appointed to head the divisions, and often stops there.

Some kind of co-ordination between units is always needed in order to take advantage of central resources. This is done through control of performance; the chief co-ordination mechanism, in other words, is standardization of result reporting.

5 *Adhocracy*

None of the contours discussed thus far provides an environment conducive to sophisticated innovation or creative problem-solving. The Machine Bureaucracy and Professional Bureaucracy are both performance oriented, not problem oriented, structures. The creation of an environment for problem-solving calls for a fifth and very special type of structure that can bring together experts from different disciplines in smoothly functioning *ad hoc* project groups.

The Adhocracy is very much an organic structure with a low degree of behaviour formalization, a high degree of horizontal work specialization based on training, and a tendency to group specialists in functional units for purposes of internal administration but in small market-based project groups to do the actual work. It encourages mutual give and take, which is its most important co-ordination mechanism. Invention implies the breaking of old moulds, so an innovative adhocracy must eschew any form of standardization.

MINTZBERG'S STRATEGY ANALYSIS

In 1984, Henry Mintzberg wrote a famous article on business strategy entitled 'Strategy in Three Modes'. It marked the start of a new approach to issues of strategy, as its publication coincided with the emergence of the new insights into the crucial factors for success in business and industry that began to gain ground in the mid-1970s.

Mintzberg distinguishes between three different kinds of strategy development:

Planning model

1 Strategy determination is a deliberate, fully conscious and controlled thought process.
2 This model views strategy as a process of planning. The result is relatively standardized, and is usually expressed as a position.
3 This model designates the Chief Executive Officer, supported by a planning staff, as the chief architect responsible for designing the strategy of the organization.
4 The model assumes that strategy implementation will follow strategy determination in a specified time-frame.
5 The planning process will produce fully developed strategies, which will be formulated and communicated in various ways.
6 This classical model assumes the existence of central staffs and aims at a strategic position or portfolio strategies.

Entrepreneurial-type vision model

1 Strategy formulation is a semi-conscious process which takes place in the mind of the entrepreneurial leader.

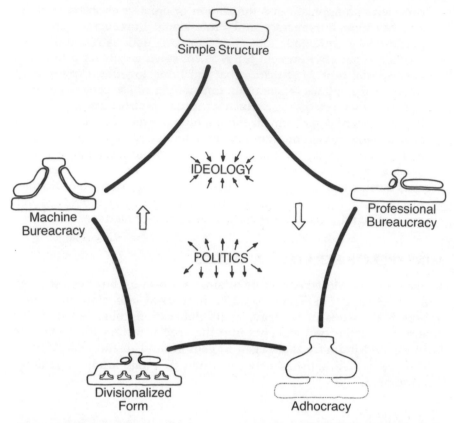

Figure 33 Mintzberg's five structures. Henry Mintzberg maintains that in every organization there are forces pushing it in different directions. The broad arrows in the figure symbolize the changes. The clusters of small arrows show that ideology is cohesive while politics is divisive.

In the Simple Structure at the top, which Mintzberg represents by a simple symbol, the top person has power over all decisions. Both internal organization and external environment support this structure. This is the first stage of an organization, for example a family firm with a dozen employees.

Organizations evolve into different forms, represented in the figure by symbols of growing complexity. The antithesis of the Simple Structure is the Machine Bureaucracy, where the technocrats have taken over and which is co-ordinated by specialization, extreme rationalization and standardization of work routines. The analysts are the important people here; the role of top management is mainly supervisory.

2 Long experience of trade logic and deep insight into trends enable him or her to formulate a vision, a scenario, of which way the business will have to go in the future.

3 The vision serves as an umbrella under which specific decisions can be made and detailed plans and activities developed.

4 The vision must remain informal and personal to preserve its fertility and flexibility.

Learning-by-experience model

1 Strategy determination is an evolutionary process of a repetitive nature, requiring mutual give-and-take.
2 Strategy is a pattern generated by impulses from the outside world received as strategy is implemented.
3 Strategy is sculpted. The strategist must approach its creation with great sensitivity and must be constantly ready to reconsider the path s/he has chosen.
4 Strategies can arise from the dynamics of an organization; embraced by a large number of people, they can fertilize and infuse the behaviour of the whole organization.
5 The process of fertilization may be either spontaneous or managed. The latter involves a smaller degree of control than that required to identify the emergence of strategies and intervene as necessary.

In the field of strategy, Henry Mintzberg is a member of the group that reacted against the way the planning technocracy, especially in the United States, had, so to speak, claimed the exclusive right to formulate strategic issues. (A technocrat is a person who takes a strictly rational economic or technical approach without regard to human values.) According to Mintzberg and others, this had led to the deprecation of visionary leadership and had given a distorted picture of the true nature of strategic management. Mintzberg's views on strategy are included here because he has exercised a powerful influence, especially in the United States, on new thinking in the field during the 1980s.

MYSIGMA PROFITABILITY GRAPH

The Swedish consultant firm Mysigma specializes in capital rationalization, that is in ways and means of minimizing capital tied up in inventory. Mysigma has devised a graph to show this.

The graph (Figure 34) shows the relationship between profit margin and rate of capital turnover. It admirably illustrates the value of simultaneously manipulating the three variables that determine profitability:

1 Reduction of tied-up capital to speed capital turnover.
2 Reduction of cost mass to increase profit margin.
3 Increasing profit margin by increasing prices.

There are three kinds of capital:

• fixed assets

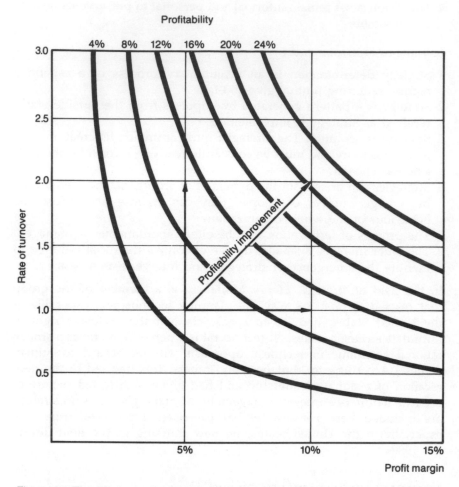

Figure 34 The Mysigma Profitability Graph. It illustrates how profitability can be improved through a higher rate of turnover and/or by better profit margins. The result is an upward movement on the profitability curve.

- inventory
- bills receivable

Whereas traditional cash management theory emphasizes bills receivable, Mysigma's approach is based on cutting down on the capital tied up in inventory. Lately, too, there has been a growth of interest in fixed asset capital, of which real estate is an important component.

The cost side of the graph comprises:

- variable unit costs, dependent on the volume of production
- fixed capacity costs, independent of the volume of production

Interest on fixed assets is generally reckoned as a fixed cost, while interest on inventory and bills receivable is classed under variable costs.

Manipulating the value variable in an attempt to increase revenues more than the added cost of added value is generally called business development. It actually involves businesslike risk-taking, and has been a subject of attention in recent years. Research, using the PIMS database and other sources, has shown that an improvement in customer-perceived quality is reflected by an increase in margins. This means that the additional revenue earned by an improvement in quality (upward differentiation) exceeds the additional cost of achieving the improvement.

The revenue side falls into two parts:

- revenue per unit sold
- number of units sold

NORDIC SCHOOL OF SERVICE MARKETING

The Nordic School of Service Marketing has developed the model shown in Figure 35. It covers outward marketing, but does not explicitly deal with the issues of how to understand the market and how to make market analyses.

Quality

The long-term goals of any company's marketing should be to achieve profitability and enhance the company's profile. The way customers perceive the quality, normally in relation to price, of goods, services and other transactions that constitute their dealings with the company affects both their buying behaviour and their perception of the company itself – its profile. The better the quality as customers perceive it, the greater their inclination to buy (and, most important, to come back and buy again), and the better the company's profile will be.

Customer-perceived quality is influenced by both expectations and actual experience of contacts with the company. The closer experience corresponds to expectations, the better the perceived quality. Be it noted that perceived quality may be good on different levels: the level of quality depends, again, on the needs, wishes and demands of consumers in a given segment.

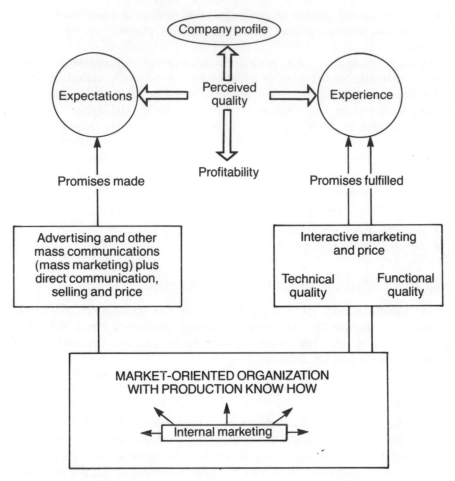

Figure 35 The Nordic School of Service Marketing has constructed this result-oriented, long-term marketing model.

Source: Totalkommunikation by Christian Grönroos and Dan Rubinstein

Expectations

Expectations are determined by the promises a company makes in various ways to its customers. These promises are made mainly through traditional marketing activities like advertising and other forms of mass communication, personal selling and sales promotion, special price offers, and public relations exercises. In addition, there is influence from the company's profile as discerned from previous contacts and from external factors like word-of-mouth, references and reputation.

In terms of service-oriented marketing, we can say that expectations are aroused mainly by the company's traditional marketing function, which on consumer markets can be characterized as primarily a mass-marketing function, whereas on business-to-business markets the personal selling element is an additional influence of greater or lesser magnitude.

Experience

Experience in relations between a company and its customers is largely controlled by factors other than those that control expectations.

In the first place, experience depends on the technical quality of the article, service or system the customer buys. Technical quality can be defined as what the customer gets in the way of a technical solution to some problem when he buys and consumes or otherwise uses a product, a service or a system of products and services.

In the second place, experience is influenced by the functional quality of relations between the company and its customers.

Functional quality is a matter of how the relationship works from the customer's standpoint. It may, for example, have to do with how the representatives of a household or corporate customer judge the behaviour of the people they come into contact with. It also has to do with their views on the system of delivery, invoicing and dealing with complaints. Yet another aspect is the physical environment in which the contacts take place, for example the interior of a shop, a delivery van, means of transport, tools and documentation.

The level of functional quality depends on how market-oriented the company's resources are in its customer relations. In service marketing and service-oriented business-to-business marketing, we speak in this context of a company's interactive marketing function.

PORTER'S COMPETITIVE ANALYSIS

Thanks to his writings and his ability to spellbind an audience, Michael Porter, a Professor at the Harvard Business School, has been a powerful influence even in those areas which are simply compilations of prior knowledge.

That category includes competitive analysis, which occupied a prominent place in the strategic planning that was so strongly favoured in an earlier era. Running a business was often viewed in terms of game theory, which conjured up analogies with warfare, chess and other phenomena that lend themselves to overview. The actors were regarded as pieces in a game, and the job of management consisted largely in trying to assess how other actors were thinking and evaluating the situation.

Components of competitive analysis

The object of competitive strategy, according to Porter, is to position your own company in such a way that it can exploit its advantages to the full.

From this it follows that an in-depth analysis of the competition is an important element of strategy formulation. The purpose of the analysis is to gain an appreciation of what changes in strategy your competitors are likely to make:

1 What are your competitors' chances of succeeding?
2 How is a given competitor likely to react to conceivable strategic moves by other companies?
3 How are competitors likely to react to the many changes in the industry and the outside world that could conceivably occur?
4 Whom in the industry do you want to challenge, and with what weapons?
5 What does a competitor hope to accomplish by his strategic move, and how should you view it?
6 What areas should you steer clear of to avoid provoking counter-measures that might cause you pain or expense?

Competition analysis, like any other kind of strategy analysis, is hard work. It demands extensive research and many of the facts you need are hard to unearth.

According to Porter, there are four diagnostic components of competition analysis:

1 Future goals.
2 Assumptions.
3 Current strategy.
4 Opportunities.

With a fair understanding of these four components, you can make predictions concerning the reaction profiles of your competitors. Such a profile is defined by the key questions in the figure.

I should now like to comment on Porter's definitions of the four components.

Future goals

Knowledge of goals makes it possible to predict how satisfied a given competitor is with his present position and financial results. On this basis you can judge the probability of that competitor having to change his strategy and react to events that affect him.

Knowledge of competitors' goals can also help you to predict reactions to changes in the strategic picture. Some such changes may threaten a particular competitor. Diagnosis of competitors' goals should further include qualitative factors such as market leadership, technological position and social status.

Assumptions

Conceptions, again according to Porter, fall into two categories:

1 The competitor's perception of himself.
2 The competitor's assumptions concerning the industry and the other companies in it.

Every company operates according to certain assumptions concerning its own circumstances. It may for example regard itself as the leader in its field, a low-cost manufacturer, the company with the best sales force, or whatever. Such assumptions often influence the way a company behaves and reacts to events.

Current strategy

According to Porter, a competitor's strategy ought to be defined as the operative programme laid down for every functional area of his company and the way in which he tries to co-ordinate the various functions. A strategy may be explicit or implicit, but is always there in some form.

Opportunities

Competitors' opportunities complete the diagnostic puzzle. Their goals, assumptions and strategies all affect the probability, timing, nature and intensity of their reactions.

Porter then goes on to discuss strengths, weaknesses, opportunities and threats. When he proceeds from the diagnostic to the therapeutic, his synthesis is brief. He holds that on the basis of competitors' future goals, assumptions, current strategies and opportunities, one can begin to ask the key questions that give a picture of competitors' likely reactions to various situations.

The reader who is interested in learning more is referred to Michael Porter's book *Competitive Strategy*.

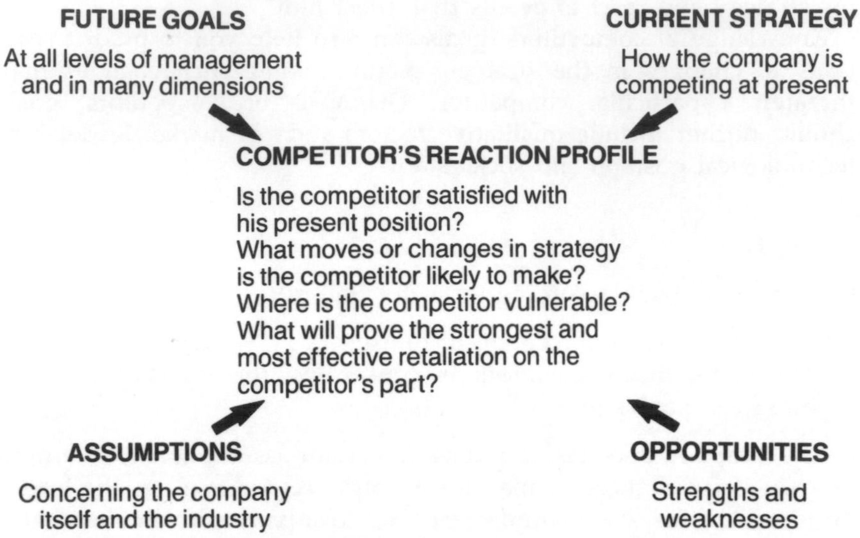

FUTURE GOALS

At all levels of management
and in many dimensions

CURRENT STRATEGY

How the company is
competing at present

COMPETITOR'S REACTION PROFILE

Is the competitor satisfied with
his present position?
What moves or changes in strategy
is the competitor likely to make?
Where is the competitor vulnerable?
What will prove the strongest and
most effective retaliation on the
competitor's part?

ASSUMPTIONS

Concerning the company
itself and the industry

OPPORTUNITIES

Strengths and
weaknesses

Figure 36 Porter's definitions of the components of competition analysis.

PORTER'S FIVE COMPETITIVE FORCES

Michael Porter has identified the five competitive forces that determine profitability in an industry:

1 Entry of new competitors into the arena.
2 Threat from substitutes based on other technology.
3 Bargaining power of buyers.
4 Bargaining power of suppliers.
5 Competition between companies already established on the market.

Competitive strategies (business strategies) are derived from an understanding of the rules of ccmpetition that govern an industry and determine its attractiveness. The ultimate goal of competitive strategy is to influence those rules in one's own company's favour. The rules of competition can be described by the five competitive forces shown in Figure 37.

Potential entrants

The establishment of a new company in an industry implies an increment of capacity. This can result in price-cutting, or inflate the cost structures of companies in the industry and reduce their profitability. According to Porter there are six major obstacles to would-be entrants:

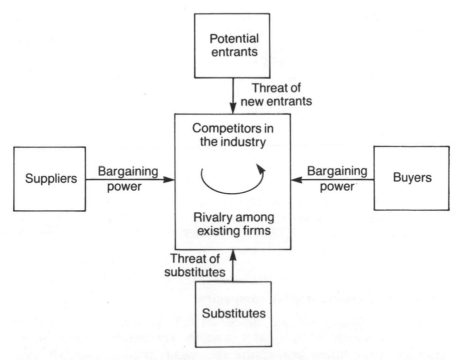

Figure 37 Porter's five competitive forces. According to Porter, these determine the profitability of an industry and are crucial to its attractiveness.

1 Economics of scale, which mean that the unit cost of a product or service falls with rising volume per unit of time. The economies of scale deter new entrants by forcing them either to start out on a massive scale, which calls for heavy investment, or to risk crushing retaliation from established companies in the industry.
2 Differentiation of production, which means that established companies have known trade marks and enjoy brand loyalty as a result of marketing efforts or tradition. The new entrant must spend a lot of money to break down existing loyalties.
3 Need for capital, which makes it difficult to get started in cases where it takes a large capital stake to be able to compete. This hurdle naturally grows higher with the uncertainty factor. Capital may be needed not only for production but also to extend credit to customers, build up stocks and cover initial losses. Rank Xerox set up an effective barrier to new entrants in the office copier business by renting machines instead of selling them, thereby upping the capital ante for potential competitors.
4 Conversion costs, a one-off expense for buyers who switch

suppliers. Conversion costs may include retraining of personnel, new production equipment, need for technical service, new product design and risk of production stoppages.

5 Lack of distribution channels, which may make it impossible for new entrants to establish a foothold in the trade. New actors must resort to cut-price offers, subsidizing advertising and other inducements to persuade established distributors and outlets to accept their products, thereby cutting into their profit margins.

6 Other cost obstacles unrelated to the economies of scale may, according to Porter, arise from advantages enjoyed by established companies in the industry. These include:

- patented product technology
- access to raw materials on favourable terms
- advantageous location
- priority claim on Government subsidies
- lead in know-how or experience

Competition among existing companies

Competition among existing companies follows well-worn procedures for gaining a more advantageous position. These include tactical exercises like price offers, advertising campaigns, product launches, customer service and warranties.

Rivalry arises, according to Porter, when one or more competitors are in a squeeze or see an opportunity to improve their position. The intensity of competition in an industry can range from polite or gentlemanly through keen to fierce or cut-throat.

Porter points to a number of factors that determine the intensity of competition:

- many competitors or competitors of comparable strength
- slow growth rate in the industry
- high fixed manufacturing or inventory costs
- no differentiation (no conversion costs)
- quantum jumps in capacity
- competitors of different kinds
- high strategic value
- high exit barriers

Substitutes

All the companies in a given industry compete, in a broad sense, with other industries that deliver substitute products. Substitutes limit the profit potential of an industry by putting a ceiling on the prices that companies in the industry can ask without losing profitability. To identify substitutes, one must look around for other products that can perform the same function as one's own. This can sometimes be difficult, leading the analyst into areas that are apparently far removed from the industry concerned.

Bargaining power of buyers

Buyers compete with an industry by exerting a downward pressure on its prices, negotiating for higher quality or better service, and playing off one competitor against another, all at the expense of the industry's profitability. The strength of each of the industry's most important groups of buyers depends on a number of factors that characterize the market situation.

A group of buyers is powerful if it meets the following criteria:

- it is concentrated, or buys large volumes in relation to the volume of suppliers' sales
- the products it buys from the industry represent an important proportion of its own costs or volume of purchases
- the products it buys from the industry are standardized or undifferentiated
- it is not sensitive to conversion costs
- its profit margins are small
- the industry's product is not crucial to the quality of the buyers' own products or services
- it is well informed

Bargaining power of suppliers

Suppliers can put pressure on the actors in an industry by threatening to raise the price or cut the quality of the goods and services they deliver. Suppliers in a position of strength can thus reduce the profitability of an industry that is not in a position to cover cost increases by raising its own prices. The factors that make suppliers powerful tend to reflect those that make groups of buyers powerful.

A group of suppliers is powerful if it meets the following criteria:

- it is dominated by a few companies and is more concentrated than the industry it sells to
- it is not forced to compete with substitutes for the products it sells to the industry
- the industry concerned is not one of its most important customers
- its products are crucial to the industry's business

- its products are differentiated
- it poses a credible threat of forward integration, that is of establishing itself in the industry

According to Porter, a company can identify its own strengths and weaknesses in relation to its industry by analysing the forces that affect competition in the industry and their underlying causes.

PORTER'S GENERIC STRATEGIES

The term generic means universally applicable or derived from certain basic postulates.

In *Competitive Strategy* (1980), Michael Porter presents three basic generic strategies for improving competitive power. A company that wants to achieve a competitive edge must make a strategic choice to avoid becoming 'all things to all men'.

The three basic strategies are:

- cost leadership
- differentiation
- focus

To achieve cost leadership, a company must keep its costs lower than its competitors'. To achieve differentiation, it must be able to offer something that is perceived as unique of its kind. By focus, Porter means that a company concentrates its efforts on a specific group of buyers or a specific segment of a product group or a specific geographical market.

Cost leadership is perhaps the most distinct of the three generic strategies. It means that a company aims to be the low-cost producer in its industry. The company has a broad scope of delivery and serves many segments within its industry. This breadth is often a key factor in its cost leadership. The nature of the cost advantage varies according to the structure of the industry; it may be a matter of economies of scale, superior technology or access to raw materials.

Low-cost production involves much more than just moving down the EXPERIENCE CURVE. A low-cost producer must find and exploit every opportunity to gain a cost advantage. The commonest situation is one where a producer is selling standard products with no added values, where staple goods are involved and where the distribution chain is strong.

Porter goes on to point out that a cost leader cannot afford to ignore the principles of differentiation. If buyers do not regard the product

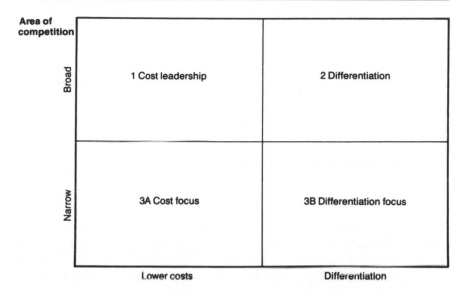

Figure 38 Porter's generic strategies. Porter's four-field matrix shows the choice of strategies. Square 1 is occupied, for example, by the major European small car manufacturers who achieve price leadership through large volume and low unit costs. Volvo could be placed in square 2, while BMW, which makes big luxury cars for a small market that is not sensitive to price, is in square 3B.

as comparable or acceptable, the cost leader will be forced to discount prices to undercut his competitors, thereby losing his cost advantage.

Porter concludes from this that a cost leader must be on a par with his competitors, or at least within reach of the principles of differentiation.

Differentiation means, according to Porter, that a company strives to be unique in its industry in some respect that is appreciated by a large number of buyers. It selects one or more qualities that many of the industry's customers consider important, and positions itself to satisfy customers' needs. The reward for this type of behaviour is that the products command a higher price.

It follows from this line of reasoning that differentiation variables are specific to each industry. Differentiation can be sought in the product itself, in the method of delivery, in the method of marketing or in some other factor. A company that goes in for differentiation must therefore always seek ways to achieve cost-effectiveness, because otherwise it risks losing its competitive edge through a disadvantageous cost position.

The difference between cost leadership and differentiation is that the former can be achieved in only one way, that is through an advantageous cost structure, whereas differentiation can be achieved in many ways.

Focus is the third generic strategy. It differs radically from the other two in that it is based on the choice of a narrow field of competition within the industry.

Focusing consists in choosing a segment within an industry and adapting your strategy to serve that segment more efficiently than your competitors do. By optimizing the strategy for selected target groups, the focuser tries to achieve a competitive edge *vis-à-vis* the selected group.

There are two kinds of focus strategy. With the COST FOCUS approach, a company tries to gain a cost advantage in its chosen segment. With DIFFERENTIATION FOCUS, on the other hand, it tries to set itself apart from other companies in its industry. In this way the focuser can gain a competitive edge by concentrating on exclusive segments of the market. The breadth of the target group is naturally a question of degree rather than kind, but the very essence of focusing lies in exploiting a narrow target group that differs from the rest of the industry's customers.

According to Porter, any one of the three generic strategies can be used as an effective means of acquiring and keeping a competitive edge.

Firms that are stuck in the middle

The following is an extract from Michael Porter's *Competitive Strategy*:

> The three generic strategies are alternative, viable approaches to dealing with the competitive forces. The converse of the previous discussion is that the firm failing to develop its strategy in at least one of the three directions – a firm that is 'stuck in the middle' – is in an extremely poor strategic situation. This firm lacks the market share, capital investment, and resolve to play the low-cost game, the industry-wide differentiation necessary to obviate the need for a low-cost position, or the focus to create differentiation or a low-cost position in a more limited sphere.
>
> A firm stuck in the middle is almost guaranteed on low profitability. It either loses the high-volume customers who demand low prices or must bid away its profits to get this business away from low-cost firms. Yet it also loses high-margin business – the cream – to the firms who are focused on high-margin targets or have achieved differentiation overall. The firm stuck in the middle also

probably suffers from a blurred corporate culture and a conflicting set of organizational arrangements and motivation system.

The firm stuck in the middle must make a fundamental strategic decision. Either it must take the steps necessary to achieve cost leadership or at least cost parity, which usually involve aggressive investments to modernize and perhaps the necessity to buy market share, or it must orient itself to a particular target (focus) or achieve some uniqueness (differentiation). The latter two options may very well involve shrinking in market share and even in absolute sales.

(Porter 1980: 41)

Risks of cost leadership

A cost leader is under constant pressure to keep its position, which means that it must invest in modern equipment, ruthlessly discard obsolete assets, resist the temptation to widen its product range and stay alert for technical improvements. Cost reductions are by no means an automatic consequence of large volume, nor is it possible to enjoy all the advantages of economies of scale without constant vigilance.

There are several hazards to beware of:

- technological advances that negate the value of existing investments and know-how
- new competitors or followers who gain the same cost advantage by imitation or investment in modern equipment
- failure to detect the need for changes in the product or the market as a result of being over-preoccupied with cost issues
- cost inflation, which erodes the company's ability to maintain a big enough price differential to offset competitors' goodwill or other advantages of differentiation

Risks of differentiation

Differentiation has its own hazards:

- the cost gap between the differentiated company and its low-cost competitors may be too wide to be bridged by the specialties, service or prestige that the differentiated company can offer its customers
- the buyer's need for the differentiated factor may diminish; this is apt to happen as buyers grow more knowledgeable
- imitation may blur the perceptible difference, a common phenomenon in maturing industries

The first of these risks is so great that it merits a special comment.

A company can differentiate its product, but the differentiation can only overcome so much difference in price. So if a differentiated company lags too far behind in cost due to either changes in technology or sheer inattention, a low-cost company can get into a strong attack position. Thus Kawasaki and other Japanese motor-cycle manufacturers were able to attack differentiated producers of heavy motorcycles like Harley Davidson and Triumph by offering substantial cost savings to buyers.

Risks of focusing

Focusing involves risks of a different kind:

- increasing cost differentials between broad producers and the focusing company may eliminate the cost advantages of serving a narrow target group or outweigh the differentiation achieved through focusing
- the difference between the kinds of products and services demanded by the strategic target group and the market at large may grow less
- competitors may find target groups within the focused company's target group and succeed better with their new venture

Many practical businessmen and women consider Porter's theories far too general to be of real explanatory value in a real-life situation. Nevertheless, it remains true that the balance between the creation of customer-perceived value and price is a central question, and that is what Porter's theory of generic strategies is all about (*see also* VALUE in the glossary).

PROBLEM DETECTION STUDIES (PDS)

The problem detection study (PDS) technique is not a strategy model, but it does play a decisive part in the current trend of strategic thinking towards a thorough understanding of customer need structures.

The PDS process involves starting with a number of in-depth interviews in order to formulate the problems connected with the use of a given product or service. The rough list of problems is then used as a basis for polling a large number of respondents. The responses are crunched in a computer.

Although this technique does not get to the root of the customer need structures, it does often offer a good grasp of the problems that customers experience in using a particular product or service. The results of a problem detection study can often be utilized to make a company more competitive.

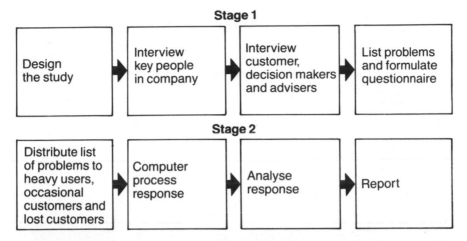

Stage 1

| Design the study | Interview key people in company | Interview customer, decision makers and advisers | List problems and formulate questionnaire |

Stage 2

| Distribute list of problems to heavy users, occasional customers and lost customers | Computer process response | Analyse response | Report |

Figure 39 Problem detection study. The PDS process comprises two stages with a total of eight steps. It is based on making in-depth interviews and using the response to identify and formulate problems in order to market products more effectively.

PRODUCT/MARKET MATRIX

The Product/Market Matrix, often called the Product/Market Certainty Matrix, is a classic model in strategy development; its origins cannot be definitely identified.

The matrix is a practical tool for sorting products and markets (read customer categories) with reference to the degree of uncertainty as to sales potential or the possibility of penetrating a given market with a given product. Experience tells that it is much harder to sell completely unrelated products to existing customers than it is to sell products linked to the existing range. Products in this context means both goods and services.

Similarly, experience suggests that it is easier to sell an existing range of products to customer categories close to those who are already buying than to sell to entirely new markets. An example is IBM's attempt to establish itself on the office copier market and Rank Xerox's reversed-sign attempt to establish itself on the personal computer market.

In advanced applications, the squares of the matrix can be assigned probabilities which are multiplied by potential sales volume. This serves to quantify a planned situation with regard to sales or business development.

A common error associated with the use of this matrix is to treat the market concept simply as an abstraction without taking the trouble to personify it. You cannot treat a shipyard as a single customer and

	Present products	New but related products	Entirely new products
Present market	90%	60%	30%
New but related market	60%	40%	20%
Entirely new market	30%	20%	10%

Figure 40 The Product/Market Matrix shows how the probability of successful selling diminishes with increasing distance from existing main product lines and main markets. The classic example is the car rental agent whose corporate mission was to rent cars to businessmen (left-hand square in top row). When business prospered, he decided to branch out and started renting cars to businessmen's wives (left-hand square in middle row). That was not so successful; the result was only 60 per cent. He was even less successful – only 30 per cent – when he started selling holiday travel for businessmen (right-hand square in top row).

draw conclusions about potential sales of ships' propellers, airline tickets and consultancy services, because these products and services are bought by different individuals who have no contact with each other.

The PM Matrix is also used to subdivide a business into markets and market segments or products and services. The sorting process and its results can provide valuable clues to the orientation of business: which categories of customers to concentrate on and which to ignore, and what parts of the product range ought to be developed or cut back.

Meteoric careers in business often give rise to situations where an executive does not know enough about the types of customer to whom different items in a product range are sold. In that kind of situation, the sorting process itself is of great value. The matrix also offers a means of keeping track of trends in markets/market segments and products/groups of products.

PROFILE STUDY

A profile is the sum of the characteristics by which a company or part of a company is known to an important target group. A corporate profile is the image a company or its products has in the eyes of the target group.

Profile studies have been used most often by companies that sell consumer goods and by service and consultancy companies, whose product is of a more abstract nature.

Examples of consumer goods for which profile studies have been undertaken are fast-turnover products like toothpaste and shampoo. In the case of consumer durables, such studies have been run for cars, TV sets and houses.

There have been corporate profile studies for service-producing companies like banks and airlines, and for consultant firms in the fields of data, management and law.

The outside world's perception of what a consultancy firm stands for is crucial to customers' choice of consultants, so awareness of one's own profile is an invaluable guide to action.

In recent years the profile study has also begun to be applied to producers of industrial hardware. This has grown as a broader spectrum of business has become more market-oriented.

Market orientation means that companies start to study the underlying need structures that control demand and use the knowledge thus acquired to make changes that will improve their ability to satisfy customers' needs. Technocratic industrial management structures are traditionally more production oriented and have therefore been less inclined to take a genuine interest in customers' wishes and customers' perception of the company, that is its profile.

The graph in figure 41 illustrates how three management consultancy firms are viewed by their markets. It is an actual example of a testography project run by Testologen AB in Sweden.

PROFIT IMPACT OF MARKETING STRATEGY (PIMS)

Like many other phenomena in the field of strategy, PIMS can trace its origins back to General Electric in the latter half of the 1960s.

PIMS represents a bold attempt to synthesize all the variables that affect a company's long-term profitability. Using some thirty variables, it claims to be able to give 67 per cent of the total explanation of a company's success.

PIMS consists of a database covering nearly 3,000 business units, mainly in North American and European companies. It contains all the variables on each of these companies, and by subscribing to PIMS you can compare business units in your own sphere of activity with the strategic guidelines given in the empirical PIMS material. The fact that the model is empirical is one of the great advantages of PIMS: this narrows the gap between the abstract and the concrete.

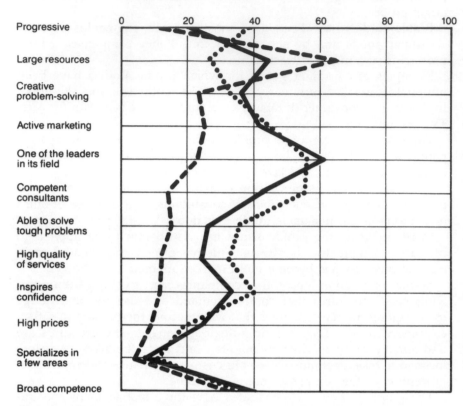

Figure 41 The market profiles of three consultancy firms. The one represented by the solid line is perceived as the market leader, but has evident difficulty in inspiring confidence in the quality of its services.

Competitive situation refers to market share and relative product quality, which is measured on the basis of both service and product variables.

Production structure refers to the amount of tied-up capital in relation to sales and in relation to added value. Profitability varies inversely with the amount of tied-up capital relative to sales or added value. Other causal variables under this heading are capacity utilization and productivity measured in terms of added value.

Market situation refers to the growth of the market, the capital intensiveness of the industry (which has a negative influence on profitability), marketing costs relative to the value of sales, and the total amount spent on purchasing. A high purchase sum generally has a negative effect on profitability.

COMPETITIVE SITUATION

Market share	+
Relative market share	+
Relative product quality	+

PRODUCTION STRUCTURE

Investment/Sales	−
Investment/Added value	−
Capacity utilization	+
Productivity	+

MARKET SITUATION

Growth	+
Capital intensiveness	−
Marketing/Sales	−
Sum of purchases	−

Figure 42 Profit Impact of Marketing Strategy. These are the decisive profitability factors for an industry – any industry – according to PIMS, which divides them into three groups. A plus sign indicates a favourable effect on profitability, a minus sign indicates an adverse effect.

The factors that have the greatest influence on profitability are, in descending order:

- capital intensiveness
- relative product quality
- relative market share
- productivity

An attractive feature of the PIMS model is that it attempts to measure relative product quality. As readers of this book will have gathered, I am convinced that the key to success in business lies in the fulfilment of customers' need structures. PIMS is the only strategy analysis system that attempts to chart how far the product satisfies need structures, except for Michael Porter's VALUE CHAIN.

The PIMS database is currently operated by the Strategic Planning Institute in Boston, Mass., with branches in other countries. One of the great advantages of the system is the high level of the discussion it generates. The conclusions may sometimes be too hastily drawn but the debate is always on the right level and concerned with essentials.

A drawback of PIMS, or rather of its interpreters, is the temptation to get caught up in a mechanistic view of companies and their development and forget the realities of business. One finds that people with a bias towards technocratic planning sometimes have a weakness for PIMS, to the detriment of the system's reputation among more business-oriented strategists.

But there is another great advantage of PIMS that must be emphasized, namely the rich body of research that is being done on the material in the PIMS database. This research is generating new ideas in many important facets of strategy.

SERVICE MANAGEMENT SYSTEM

The idea of the Service Management System emerged gradually in the course of Richard Normann's work on service organizations. According to him, the aim of the theoretical base is to integrate, but also to extend to, the model or magic formula of the service system as developed by Eiglier and Langeard, and to include the corporate mission as expounded in Normann's own book *Skapande företagsledning* (Creative Management).

Market segment refers to the special category of customer for whom the whole service system is devised.

Service concept means the benefits offered to the customer. Experience shows that the service concept often comprises highly complex combinations of values which are often difficult to analyse. Some of them are tangible, others psychological or emotional. Some are more important than others and can be classed as basic services, while others are of a more peripheral nature.

Service delivery system is equivalent to the production and distribution system of a manufacturing company, though often of a radically different kind. We shall consider the service delivery system in some depth because it is here, more often than in the formulation of the service concept, that we find a service company's unique and most innovative ideas. In analysing the service delivery system, we can distinguish three components:

1 Staff: service organizations are usually personality-intensive, and the most successful ones have devised highly creative and rigorous methods of discovering, developing and focusing human resources. They also strive to find ways to mobilize people not on their own payroll.
2 Customers: the customer plays an astonishingly complex part in a

service organization, because she/he not only receives and consumes service but also acts as a component in its production and delivery. This is one of the reasons why customers must be selected and guided just as carefully as the company's own employees.

3 Technology and physical support: services, besides being generally personality-intensive, are often capital-intensive or equipment-intensive too. It must be emphasized that modern technology, especially information technology, will become increasingly important in the service sector.

Our analysis is concerned with one special aspect of technology and physical components: the distinguishing feature of service is social interaction, and physical features, be they computerized flight-booking systems or the design of restaurant tables, play an important part in influencing social relations.

Image is regarded here as an instrument of information that management can use to influence staff, customers and other suppliers of resources whose functions and whose perceptions of the company and its development affect its position on the market and its cost-effectiveness. In the long run, of course, a company's image depends on what it actually delivers and who its customers are, but in the short term image can help to fashion a new reality.

Culture and philosophy are the overriding principles according to which management controls, maintains and develops the social process that manifests itself as delivery of service and gives value to customers. Once a superior service delivery system and a realistic service concept have been established, there is no other component so crucial to the long-term effectiveness of a service organization as its culture and philosophy. They are the things that shape and inspire the values and the morale that underlie the vitality and success of a company.

STRATEGY DEVELOPMENT MODEL

See figure 44, page 203

VALUE CHAIN

The Value Chain developed by Michael Porter represents one of the first serious attempts in the field of strategy to analyse customer need structures. Porter presented the Value Chain in his book *Competitive Advantage*, published in 1985.

Value is defined in this context as what buyers are willing to pay for what they get from suppliers. A company is profitable if the value

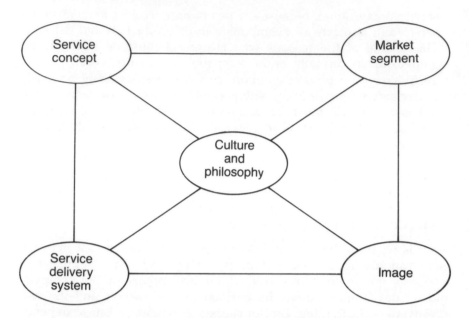

Figure 43 Service Management System. In this model we can start from market segment and proceed counterclockwise in the figure to service concept, service delivery system and image. Culture and philosophy tie the whole system together.

it generates exceeds the cost it has to pay for generating the value. Analysis of the competitive situation must therefore be based not on cost, but on value.

According to Porter, a company's competitive edge cannot be understood simply by studying the company as a whole. A competitive advantage arises out of the manifold activities which a company pursues in its design, production, marketing, delivery and supporting functions. Each of these activities can contribute to the company's relative cost position and create a basis for differentiation.

Porter places the corporate Value Chain in a greater stream of activities, which he calls the Value System; it is illustrated in figure 45.

Porter's value system

Porter's definition of value in a competitive context is the sum a buyer is willing to pay for what a supplier delivers. Value is measured as total revenue, which is a function of the price a company's product fetches and the number of units the company can sell.

Every value-generating activity involves:

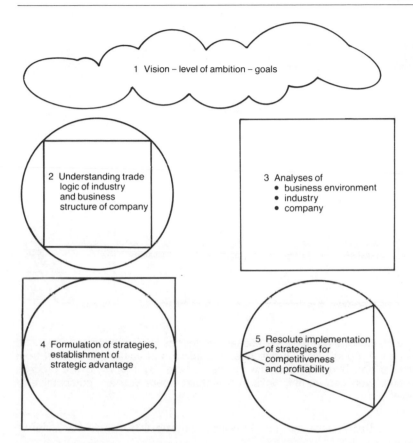

1 Vision – level of ambition – goals

2 Understanding trade
   logic of industry
   and business
   structure of company

3 Analyses of
   • business environment
   • industry
   • company

4 Formulation of strategies,
   establishment of
   strategic advantage

5 Resolute implementation
   of strategies for
   competitiveness
   and profitability

Figure 44 Strategy Development Model. In this model of the strategic process, squares symbolize analytical components, circles stand for creative components and the triangle, finally, represents the dynamic component in the actual process of implementation and learning within the organization.

- bought-in components
- human resources
- some form of technology
- information flows of various kinds

Value-generating activities can be divided into two classes: primary activities and support activities.

Primary activities are shown on the bottom line of the large arrow in Figure 45. They are the activities that result in the physical creation of a product and its sale and delivery to the buyer and after-sales market.

1 Inbound logistics comprises goods reception, warehousing, sorting,

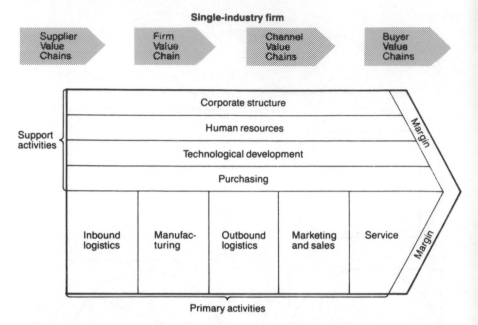

Figure 45 Value Chain. Professor Michael Porter has drawn these two diagrams to illustrate the Value Chain. It describes the addition of value to a product from raw material and purchasing to the finished article. By analysing the process step by step, you can identify links in the chain where you are competitive or vulnerable.

handling, buffer storage, stocktaking, transportation and back deliveries.

2 Manufacturing comprises all activities that convert the inflow into end products, such as machining, packaging, assembly, plant maintenance and testing.

3 Outbound logistics comprises activities concerned with shipment, warehousing and physical distribution of products to buyers. This includes order processing, scheduling, deliveries, transportation and so on.

4 Marketing and sales comprises all activities designed to persuade buyers to accept and pay for the product. This includes advertising, sales promotion, personal selling, quotation writing, choice of distribution channels and pricing.

5 Service comprises all activities designed to maintain or enhance the value of the product delivered. This includes installation, repairs, training, spare parts and product modification.

Support activities are shown on the top four lines of Figure 45. They are:

1 Corporate structure, which embraces a number of activities including management, planning, finance, accounting, legal business, relations with the public sector and quality management.
2 Human resource management, which includes the recruitment, training, development and remuneration of all categories of personnel.
3 Technological development, which affects every value-generating activity in the areas of know-how, procedures and processes.
4 Purchasing, which has to do with procurement of materials, that is the actual function of buying supplies, not the logistic flow of materials.

The author's opinion of the Value Chain is that it does a good job of emphasizing the importance of customers' value structures in contrast to the in-house cost and capital structure bias of earlier times.

One critical comment is that the explanatory value of the Value Chain is limited by the fact that it disregards the subjective and often irrational components of customers' value judgements which so often determine the choice of supplier. The analysis, moreover, is strongly deductive in so far as it strives for an understanding of the whole by chopping it up into components and seeking to understand them piecemeal. Porter says that further research based on the Value Chain should take the form of subdividing these components into even smaller parts. This appears to be a questionable approach to grasping the complex totality of a company.

Bibliography

Abell, D. E. (1980) *Defining the Business*, Englewood Cliffs, NJ: Prentice Hall.
Abell, D. E. and Hammond, J. S. (1979) *Strategic Market Planning: Problems and Analytical Approaches*, Englewood Cliffs, NJ: Prentice Hall.
Ansoff, H. I. (ed.) (1969) *Business Strategy*, London: Penguin.
Ansoff, H. I. (1965) 'Checklist for competitive and competence profiles', *Corporate Strategy*, 98–9, New York: Pelican.
Buzell, R. D. and Gail, B. T. (1987) *The PIMS Principles*, New York: Free Press.
Chandler, A. D. (1962) *Strategy and Structure*, New York.
Drucker, P. F. (1970) *Managing for Results*, Stockholm: W & W series.
Fruhan, W. E. jun. (1972) *The Fight for Competitive Advantage*, Division of Research, Harvard Graduate School of Business Administration, Cambridge, Mass.
Galbraith, J. R. and Nathanson, D. A. (1978) *Strategy Implementation: The Role of Structure and Process*, St Paul, Minn.: West.
Gardner, J. R., Rashlim, R. and Sweene, H. W. Allen (1987) *Handbook of Strategic Planning*, London: J. Wiley & Sons.
Guth, W. D. (ed.) (1985) *Handbook of Business Strategy*, Boston: Warren, Gorham & Lamont.
Harrigan, K. R. (1979) 'Strategies for declining industries', DBA thesis, Harvard Graduate School of Business Administration, Cambridge, Mass.
Haspelagh, P. (1982) 'Portfolio planning: uses and limits', *Harvard Business Review*, Jan-Feb, pp. 58–73.
Hayden, C. (1986) *The Handbook of Strategic Expertise*, New York: Free Press.
Hayes, R. H. (1985) 'Strategic planning – forward in reverse?', *Harvard Business Review*, Nov-Dec, pp. 111–19.
Hickman, C. R. and Silva, M. A. (1984) *Creating Excellence*, New York: New American (NAC Books).
Hofstede, G. (1980) *Culture's Consequences*, Beverly Hills, CA: Sage.
Hussey, D. and Lowe, P. (1990) *Key Issues in Management Training*, London: Kogan Page.
Lorange P. (1980) *Corporate Planning*, Englewood Cliffs, NJ: Prentice Hall.
Lorange, P. and Vancil, R. F. (1983) *Strategic Planning Systems*, Englewood Cliffs, NJ: Prentice Hall.
Mintzberg, H. (1987) 'Crafting strategy', *Harvard Business Review*, July-Aug, p. 66.
Ohmae, K. (1982) *The Mind of the Strategist – The Art of Japanese Business*, London: McGraw-Hill.
Pettigrew, A. (1987) *The Management of Strategic Change*, Oxford: Basil Blackwell.

Porter, M. (1980) *Competitive Strategy*, New York: Free Press.
Porter, M. (1985) *Competitive Advantage*, New York: Free Press.
Prahalad, C. K. and Doz, Eve L. (1987) *The Multinational Mission*, New York: Free Press.
Schumpeter, J. (1947) *Capitalism, Socialism and Democracy*, 2nd edn, New York: Harper.
Simon, J. A. (1971) 'On the concept of organizational goal', in H. I. Ansoff (1969) *Business Strategy*, London: Penguin.
Steiner, G. (1979) *Strategic Planning*, New York: Free Press.
Yavitz, B. and Newman, S. (1983) *Strategy in Action*, New York: Free Press.

Index